Teaching Reading Comprehension with Graphic Texts

An Illustrated Adventure

Katie Monnin

Illustrated by Rachel Bowman

by capstone professional

Teaching Reading Comprehension with Graphic Texts
An Illustrated Adventure

By Katie Monnin
and Rachel Bowman

Cover illustration: Rachel Bowman
Cover composition/design: Studio Montage

Library of Congress Cataloging-in-Publication Data
Cataloging-in-publication information is on file with the Library of Congress.
ISBN-13: 978-1-936700-58-5

Maupin House publishes professional resources for K-12 educators. Contact us for tailored, in-school training or to schedule an author for a workshop or conference. Visit www.maupinhouse.com for free lesson plan downloads.

For updated graphic novel recommendations and more on using graphic texts in the classroom, visit Katie Monnin's blog at http://teachinggraphicnovels.maupinhouse.com.

Maupin House Publishing, Inc. by Capstone Professional

1710 Roe Crest Drive
North Mankato, MN 56003
www.maupinhouse.com
800-524-0634
352-373-5546 (fax)
info@maupinhouse.com

10 9 8 7 6 5 4 3 2 1

Printed in the United States of America in Eau Claire, Wisconsin
022013 007206

TABLE OF CONTENTS

PART I: GRAPHIC TEXTS AND LITERACY TODAY

INTRODUCTION: TEACHING READING COMPREHENSION WITH GRAPHIC TEXTS

> "COMICS COMMUNICATE IN A 'LANGUAGE' THAT RELIES ON A VISUAL EXPERIENCE COMMON TO BOTH CREATOR AND AUDIENCE. MODERN READERS CAN BE EXPECTED TO HAVE AN EASY UNDERSTANDING OF THE IMAGE-WORD MIX AND THE TRADITIONAL DECIPHERING OF TEXT. COMICS CAN BE CALLED 'READING' IN A WIDER SENSE THAN THAT TERM IS COMMONLY APPLIED.... THE REGIMENS OF ART (E.G., PERSPECTIVE, SYMMETRY, BRUSH STROKE) AND THE REGIMENS OF LITERATURE (E.G., GRAMMAR, PLOT, SYNTAX) BECOME SUPERIMPOSED UPON EACH OTHER. THE READING OF THE COMIC BOOK IS AN ACT OF AESTHETIC PERCEPTION AND INTELLECTUAL PURSUIT."
>
> -WILL EISNER; COMICS AND SEQUENTIAL ART, 1985

There is a global communication revolution happening (Kress, 2003), and we are the first generation of educators to redefine what it means to teach reading comprehension in today's schools. Today's readers must be able to competently decode both print-text and image-text literacies.

Think about it for a second from a modern reader's perspective. To read is to view and to comprehend. To write is to show and ultimately communicate. Under this new definition of reading, modern literacy learners must rethink some lingering preconceptions about reading: reading in today's world is not just about holding a print-text book anymore. We're watching movies and TV, surfing the Internet, checking email, flipping through comics or graphic novels, and reading other modern literacy resources, often from our cell phones, tablets, and laptops rather than a printed book. The ability to understand multi-modal literacies—to read them—is central to literacy today.

As Eisner so clearly articulated, "the regimens of art…and the regimens of literature" have become one in today's image-dominated world. Comics and graphic novels embody this idea of reading print-text and image-text literacies together. Although Eisner and several other comics scholars were ahead of their time in pinpointing this communication revolution, their work is not finished. Comic books and graphic novels are still struggling to become an accepted, valid, respected literary format, especially in the English/language arts classroom. So, how can educators better understand graphic texts and use them to teach reading comprehension?

I present an answer to that question with this graphic memoir and educator's guide. Presented in graphic novel format, *Teaching Reading Comprehension with Graphic Texts* addresses the reasons why educators should teach graphic novels in today's language arts classrooms while providing a primer on how to read, understand, and teach the unique vocabulary and anatomy of the graphic novel format alongside traditional print-based literature and content-area selections.

With that knowledge in hand, educators will not only address Common Core State Standards for teaching multi-modal texts and comparing complex texts in various formats, they will engage learners and give them the tools they need to be fully literate and communicative in today's world.

CHAPTER 1

WHY GRAPHIC TEXTS ARE CENTRAL TO BECOMING LITERATE TODAY

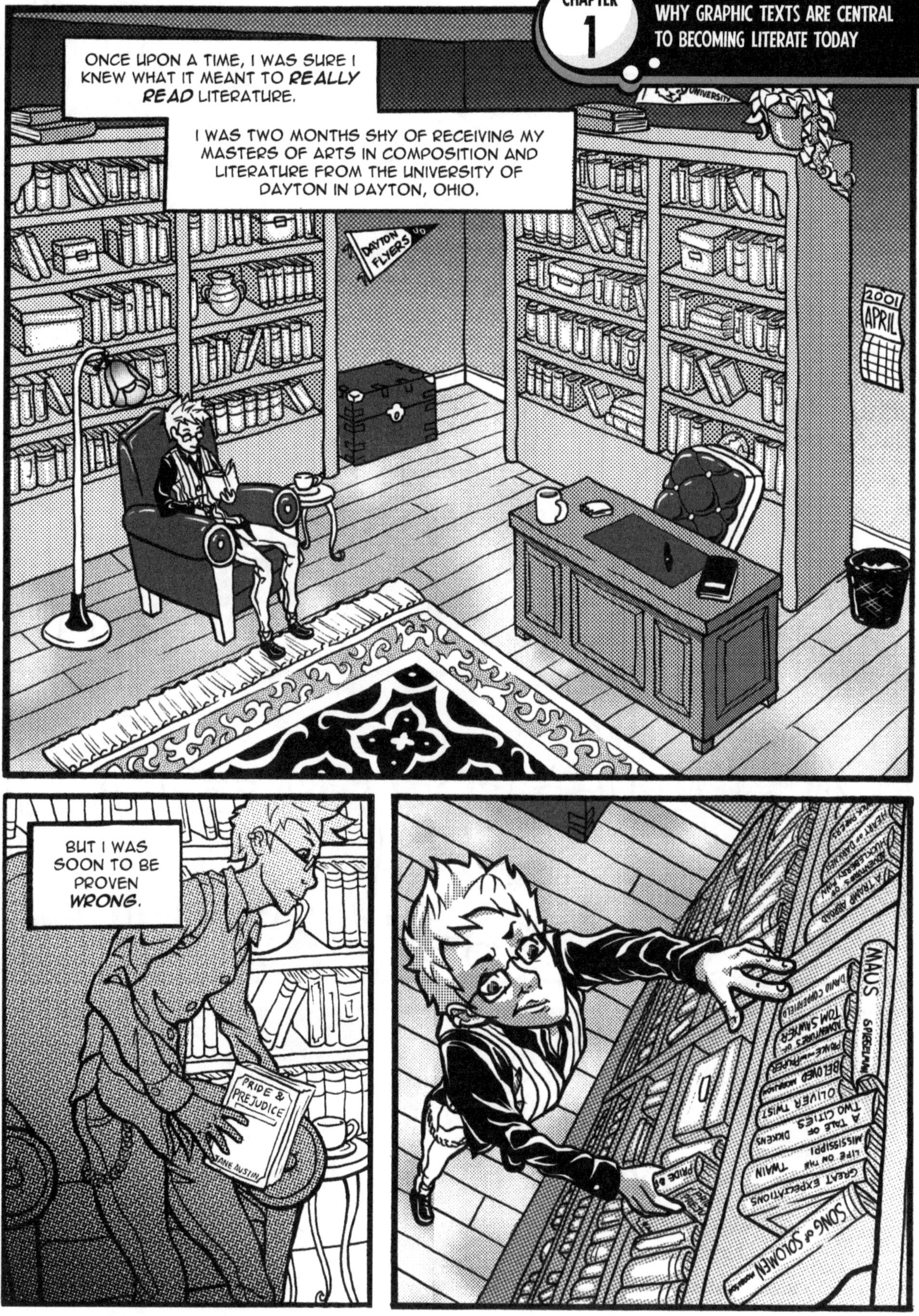

ONCE UPON A TIME, I WAS SURE I KNEW WHAT IT MEANT TO ***REALLY READ*** LITERATURE.

I WAS TWO MONTHS SHY OF RECEIVING MY MASTERS OF ARTS IN COMPOSITION AND LITERATURE FROM THE UNIVERSITY OF DAYTON IN DAYTON, OHIO.

IN FACT, AND IN HINDSIGHT, I THINK THERE WERE TWO *LITERARY MUSES* WATCHING OVER ME (AND PERHAPS A THIRD THAT WAS SOON TO JOIN THEM).
SHE THINKS SHE'S *SO SMART!*
DICKENS
AUSTEN
WAIT FOR IT!
MAUS BOOKS I & II by ART SPIEGELMAN

SPOT ON, JANE!
DICKENS
MAUS
BOOKS I & II
by
ART SPIEGELMAN
DAVID COPPERFIELD
CHARLES DICKENS

MAUS BY ART SPIEGELMAN?

SHE'S GOT IT. SHE'S GOING TO READ IT!

A GRAPHIC NOVEL?
THIS ISN'T REALLY READING!

IT'S A SORT OF *FORCE*, IF YOU WILL.

SPIEGELMAN

MAUS BOOKS I & II by ART SPIEGELMAN

UMPH!

**MAUS* CHARACTER REPRESENTATION USED WITH PERMISSION FROM ART SPIEGELMAN.

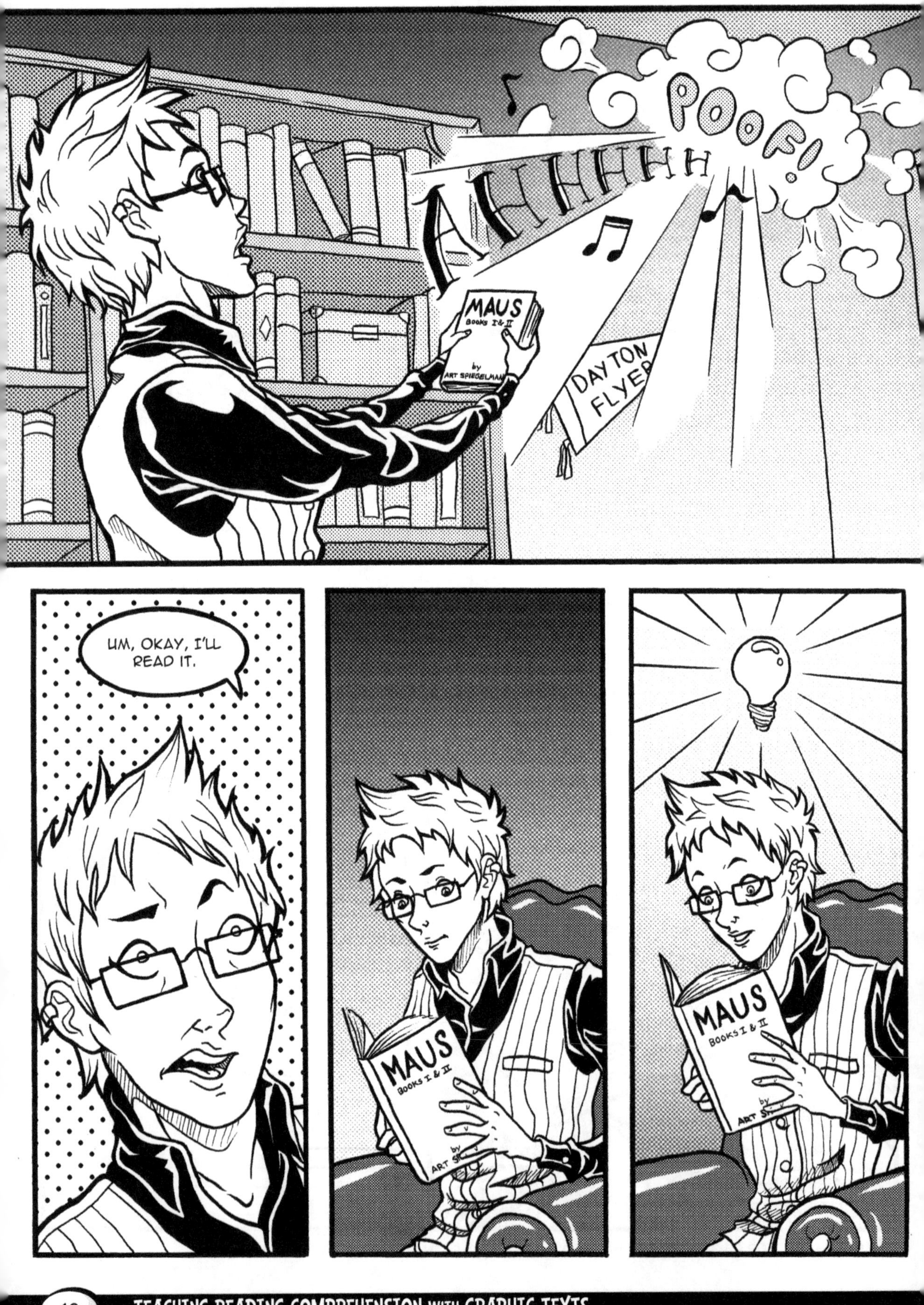

AHHHHHHH
POOF!
MAUS
BOOKS I & II
by
ART SPIEGELMAN
DAYTON FLYER

AFTER SPEAKING TO MY FRIEND WHO HAD LOANED ME ***MAUS*** SIX MONTHS EARLIER, I FOUND OUT THAT THERE WERE IN FACT ***MANY MORE*** GRAPHIC NOVELS I NEEDED TO READ; GRAPHIC NOVELS, SHE TOLD ME, I WAS NOT TO "SHOVE UP ON A SHELF SOMEWHERE." FOR THE NEXT YEAR OR SO I READ ***EVERY*** GRAPHIC NOVEL I COULD FIND.

AS I READ MORE AND MORE GRAPHIC NOVELS, COMPARING EACH WITH HOW MY BACHELOR'S AND MASTER'S EDUCATION IN ENGLISH HAD BOTH DEFINED ***LITERATURE***, I REALIZED THAT GRAPHIC NOVELS WERE, IN FACT, ***REALLY LITERATURE!***

WEBSTER'S DICTIONARY DEFINES *LITERATURE* AS...

elating to authors or scholar
work

lit·er·a·ture *n.* **1** the production of literary work, especially as an occupation **2** writings in prose or verse, especially writings having excellence of form or expression and expressing ideas of permanent or universal interest **3** the body of works produced

lithograph **2** lithograp

lith *abbr* ... ania **2** Lithuani

C.S. LEWIS, WHO BOTH WROTE AND STUDIED THE ART OF READING AND WRITING LITERATURE, DEFINES *LITERATURE* AS "ADDING TO OUR UNDERSTANDING OF REALITY AND OF LIFE."

THE VERY FIRST STANDARD FOR TEACHING READING AND WRITING, PROVIDED BY THE *INTERNATIONAL READING ASSOCIATION* (IRA) AND THE *NATIONAL COUNCIL OF TEACHERS OF ENGLISH* (NCTE), STATES THAT...

ncte.org

1. Students read a wide range of print and non-print texts to build an understanding of texts, of themselves, and of the cultures of the United States and the world; to acquire new information; to respond to the needs and demands of society and the workplace; and for personal fulfillment. Among these texts are fiction and nonfiction, classic and contemporary works.

AND WITH THESE IDEAS OF LITERATURE SWIRLING AROUND IN MY MIND, I FOUND WHAT FELT LIKE "THE MISSING LINK" BETWEEN PRINT-TEXT LITERATURE AND COMICS AND GRAPHIC NOVELS – SCOTT MCCLOUD'S *UNDERSTANDING COMICS* (HARPERCOLLINS, 1993).

Juxtaposed pictorial and other images in deliberate sequence, intended to convey information and/or to produce an aesthetic response in the viewer.

EDU-REKA! I AM REALLY READING LITERATURE WITH GRAPHIC NOVELS!
WEBSTER'S DICTIONARY DEFINE LITERATURE AS...
lit·er·a·ture n. 1
literary work, especi
2 writings in prose
writings having ex
expression and ex
permanent or univers
body of works produ
lith abb
HO BOTH WROTE AND STUDIED
THE OF READING AND WRITING
DEFINES LITERATURE AS
UNDERSTANDING OF REALITY
AND OF LIFE."
LITERATURE ADDS TO REALITY. IT DOES NOT SIMPLY DESCRIBE IT. IT ENRICHES THE NECESSARY COMPETENCIES THAT DAILY LIFE REQUIRES AND PROVIDES, AND, IN THIS RESPECT, IT IRRIGATES THE DESERTS THAT OUR LIVES HAVE ALREADY BECOME.
THE VERY FIRST STANDARD FOR TEA READING AND WRITING, PROVIDED INTERNATIONAL READING ASSOCIATI AND THE NATIONAL COUNCIL OF TEA ENGLISH (NCTE), STATES THA
ncte.org
1. Students read a wide range of pri and non-print texts to build an understanding of texts, of themse and of the cultures of the Unit States and the world; to acqui information; to respond to t demands of society and the and for personal fulfillme these texts are fiction and classic and contemporary w
THESE IDEAS OF LITERATURE SWIRL OUND IN MY MIND, I FOUND WHAT "THE MISSING LINK" BETWEEN LITERATURE AND COMICS AND NOVELS - SCOTT MCCLOUD'S UNDE DING COMICS (HARPERCOLLINS, 1993).
Juxtaposed pictorial and other images in deliberate sequence, intended to convey information and/or to produce an aesthetic response in the viewer.

RECORD YOUR THOUGHTS

**BONE* CHARACTER REPRESENTATION USED WITH PERMISSION FROM JEFF SMITH.

YOUR MISSION, SHOULD YOU CHOOSE TO ACCEPT IT, IS TO DEMYSTIFY WHAT COUNTS AS MODERN, VALUABLE CLASSROOM LITERATURE AND HELP TEACHERS BETTER UNDERSTAND THE LITERARY POTENTIAL OF THE MODERN GRAPHIC NOVEL.
AUSTEN
DIC
OUR MISSION IS TO CLARIFY THE MISUNDERSTANDINGS TEACHERS MAY HAVE ABOUT COMICS AND GRAPHIC NOVELS.
THAT SAID, NEXT SLIDE...

NOW AS WE ALL KNOW, FREDERIC WERTHAM'S 1954 PUBLICATION OF SEDUCTION OF THE INNOCENT HAS TAINTED AND POISONED THE AMERICAN UNDERSTANDING OF THE LITERARY POTENTIAL FOR BOTH COMICS AND GRAPHIC NOVELS.
NEXT SLIDE...

COUGH HACK

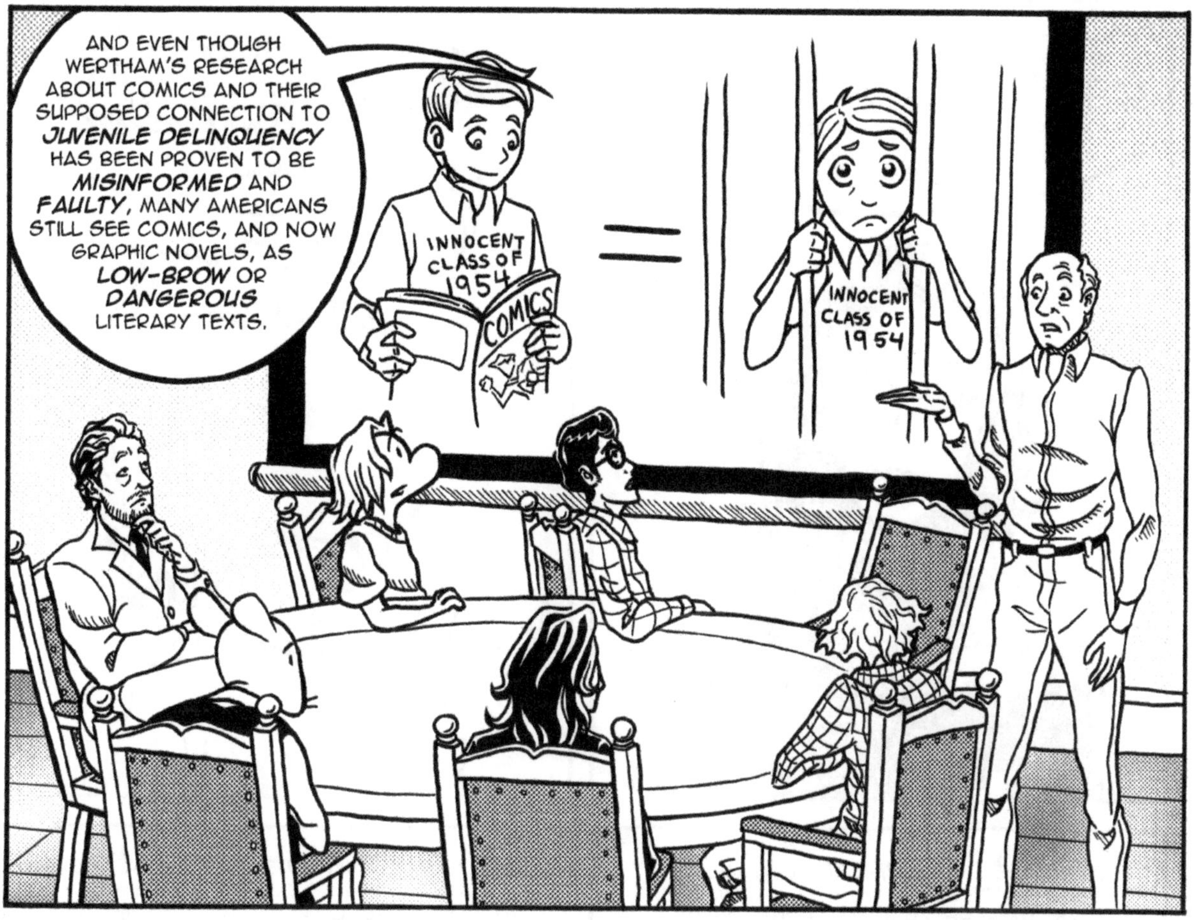

AND EVEN THOUGH WERTHAM'S RESEARCH ABOUT COMICS AND THEIR SUPPOSED CONNECTION TO ***JUVENILE DELINQUENCY*** HAS BEEN PROVEN TO BE ***MISINFORMED*** AND ***FAULTY***, MANY AMERICANS STILL SEE COMICS, AND NOW GRAPHIC NOVELS, AS ***LOW-BROW*** OR ***DANGEROUS*** LITERARY TEXTS.

INNOCENT CLASS OF 1954

COMICS

INNOCENT CLASS OF 1954

*MCCLOUD, S. (1993). *UNDERSTANDING COMICS*. NEW YORK, NY: HARPERCOLLINS.

**HARVEY PEKAR QUOTE FOUND ON WWW.BRAINYQUOTES.COM

*THIS MARJANE SATRAPI QUOTATION CAN BE FOUND IN AN IFC VIDEO FROM THE 2007 NEW YORK FILM FESTIVAL PRESS CONFERENCE (WWW.YOUTUBE.COM).

**THESE QUOTATIONS FROM JEFF SMITH CAN BE FOUND IN VIDEO INTERVIEWS WITH THE GRAPHIC NOVELIST CONDUCTED BY SCHOLASTIC: WWW.SCHOLASTIC.COM/BONE/AUTHOR.HTM.

***WITEK, J., ED. (2007). *ART SPIEGELMAN: CONVERSATIONS*. JACKSON, MS: UNIVERSITY PRESS OF MISSISSIPPI.

****CARTER, J.B. (2007). *BUILDING LITERACY CONNECTIONS WITH GRAPHIC NOVELS*. URBANA, IL: NCTE.

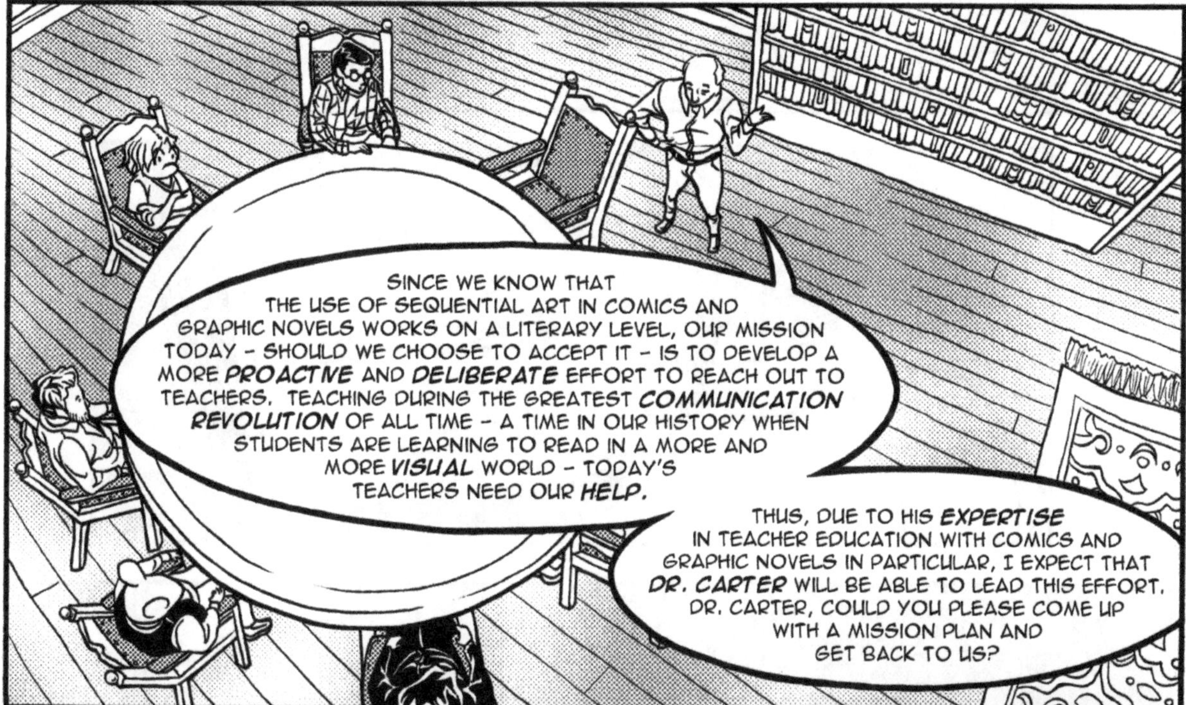

*EISNER, W. (2008). *COMICS AND SEQUENTIAL ART*. NEW YORK, NY: NORTON.

UTEP
WITH GREAT POWER COMES GREAT RESPONSIBILITY

graphic novel educators
Graphic Novels - School of Education
Graphic novels have become an essential component of library collections for both children and teenagers, and they have enormous potential for classroom use ...
Using Graphic Novels with Children and Teens: A Guide for Teachers ...
The term graphic novel is used to describe any book in a comic format that resembles a novel in length and narrative development. Works such as BONE, ...
[PDF] USING GRAPHIC NOVELS
File Format: PDF/Adobe Acrobat - Quick View
resembles a novel in length and narrative development. Are graphic novels ...
Educators Advocate for Graphic Novels in Class
Scieszka said it was educators' "mission" to bring quality graphic novels into the classroom curriculum. "Kids today are wired and stimulated in different ...
[PDF] Download a PDF of the Teacher's Guide - Random House

ROOF

The LEAGUE of EXTRAORDINARY GRAPHIC NOVEL GURUS
COMIC

RECORD YOUR THOUGHTS

PART II: LEARNING HOW TO READ AND TEACH GRAPHIC TEXTS

CHAPTER 3
PANELS

LET HER THINK WHAT SHE WANTS FOR NOW. BUT WE'VE GOTTA GET HER TO LOOK *UP*.
IF WE HAD A PENNY FOR EVERY TIME. . .
NOT NOW. ***REMEMBER:*** LOYAL, BEST FRIEND. THOSE ARE OUR ***DUTIES***.
FINE.

WHAT ARE YOU TWO THINKING? ***HEAD DOG*** HAS SPOKEN!
BARK! ARF! ARF!
DOES ***EVERYTHING*** HAVE TO HIT HER ON THE ***HEAD*** TO GET HER ATTENTION?

AUSTEN
DICKENS
!
COMIC
REALLY READING WITH GRAPHIC NOVELS

*ALL ELEVEN TYPES OF PANELS ARE EASILY ALIGNED TO THE STANDARDS FOR TEACHING THE ELEMENTS OF STORY IN LANGUAGE ARTS CLASSROOMS, SET FORTH BY BOTH THE NATIONAL COUNCIL OF TEACHERS OF ENGLISH (WWW.NCTE.ORG) AND THE INTERNATIONAL READING ASSOCIATION (WWW.READING.ORG).

THE LEAGUE OF EXTRAORDINARY
GRAPHIC NOVEL GURUS

DR. MONNIN, KATIE. YOU MAY ADDRESS ***THE LEAGUE***. NO FUNNY BUSINESS.

THE LEAGUE OF EXTRAORDINARY

DR. KATIE MONNIN
ASSISTANT PROFESSOR OF LITERACY, UNIVERSITY OF NORTH FLORIDA
REALLY READING WITH GRAPHIC NOVELS
THANK YOU ALL SO VERY MUCH FOR TAKING THE TIME TO CONSIDER MY IDEAS.

TODAY'S TOPIC: REALLY READING WITH GRAPHIC NOVELS. I WOULD LIKE TO START WITH TEACHING GRAPHIC NOVEL PANELS.
TIME TO BRING THE 'A' GAME!
OKAY, IN ORDER FOR TEACHERS TO FULLY UNDERSTAND THE LITERARY POWER OF THE GRAPHIC NOVEL, THEY FIRST NEED TO KNOW THE DEFINITION OF A PANEL...

PANEL - A VISUAL BOUNDARY THAT CONTAINS AN ELEMENT OF STORY.
WHEN I TEACH THE TERM 'PANEL,' I TRY TO COME UP WITH AN ENGAGING STORY TOPIC. FOR AN EXAMPLE TODAY, I'LL USE A STORY A GROUP OF TEACHERS AND I CREATED A WEEK AGO. AND JUST A SIDE NOTE: THE TWO SUPERHEROES IN THIS STORY HAVE REQUESTED THAT THEIR TRUE IDENTITIES REMAIN A SECRET, EVEN TO THE LEAGUE.
CLICK
EXAMPLE PANEL

ONCE EDUCATORS UNDERSTAND THE TERM 'PANEL,' I LIKE TO PAIR THEIR ALREADY EXISTING SCHEMA OF TEACHING THE ELEMENTS OF STORY (LIKE CHARACTERIZATION, SETTING, PLOT, AND SO ON) WITH PRINT-TEXT LITERATURE TO THEIR NEW KNOWLEDGE OF THE GRAPHIC NOVEL PANEL.

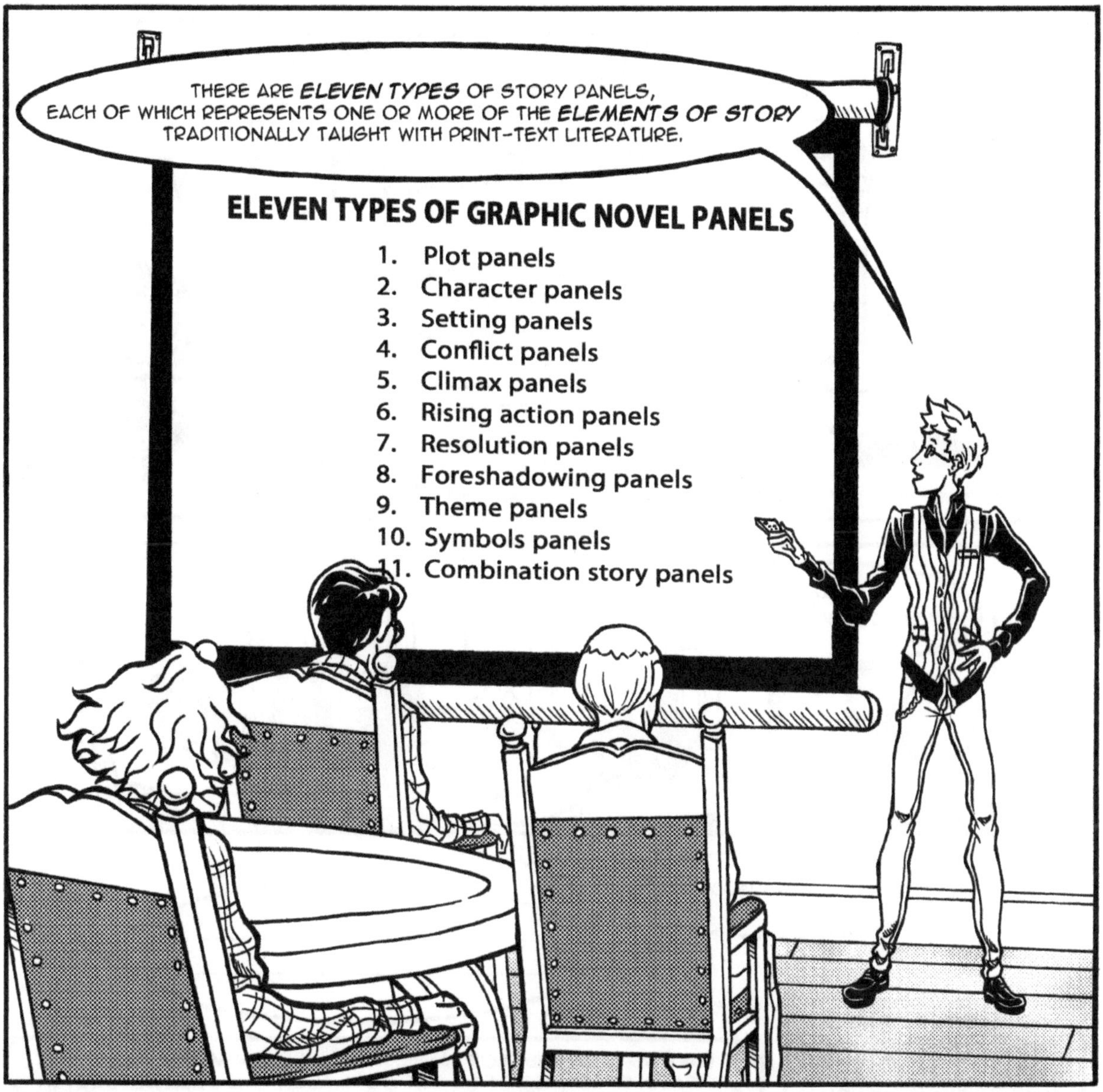

THERE ARE *ELEVEN TYPES* OF STORY PANELS, EACH OF WHICH REPRESENTS ONE OR MORE OF THE *ELEMENTS OF STORY* TRADITIONALLY TAUGHT WITH PRINT-TEXT LITERATURE.

ELEVEN TYPES OF GRAPHIC NOVEL PANELS

1. Plot panels
2. Character panels
3. Setting panels
4. Conflict panels
5. Climax panels
6. Rising action panels
7. Resolution panels
8. Foreshadowing panels
9. Theme panels
10. Symbols panels
11. Combination story panels

READER, WHAT DO ***YOU*** SEE?

____

____

BRILLIANT! SO HERE'S WHAT WE KNOW SO FAR ABOUT THE ***PLOT***: THERE'S A DISAGREEMENT. WE HAVE TWO CHARACTERS. AND JUST LIKE WITH TRADITIONAL PRINT-TEXT LITERATURE, ONE SOLID ELEMENT ***LEADS*** THE READER TO THE NEXT. IN THIS CASE, FROM A PLOT CENTERED ON A DISAGREEMENT TO A ***QUESTION*** ABOUT CHARACTERS.

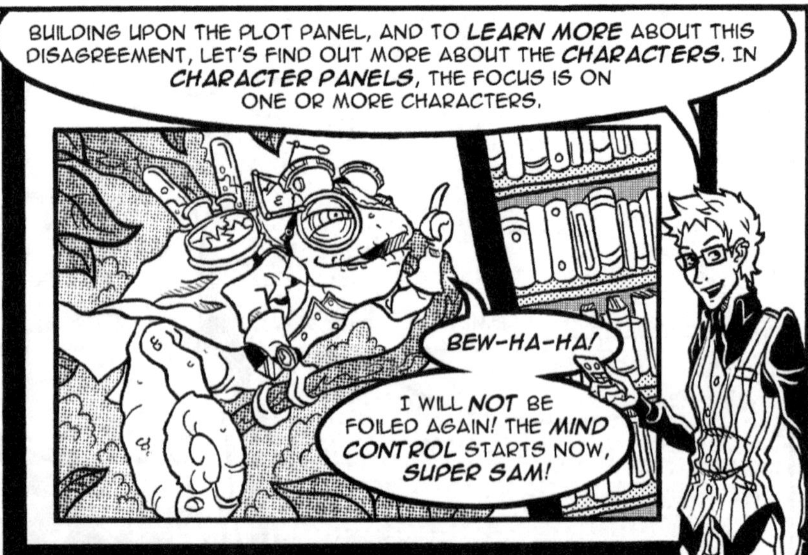

FROM THAT CHARACTER PANEL, WHAT DO WE LEARN ABOUT THE CHAMELEON AS A CHARACTER?
THE CHAMELEON SEEMS LIKE A VILLAIN.
READER, WHAT DO YOU THINK ABOUT THE CHAMELEON AS A CHARACTER?
YOU GOT IT! THIS CHAMELEON SEEMS UP TO NO GOOD. AND WHO IS SHE TALKING TO? SEEMS LIKE WE NEED ANOTHER CHARACTER PANEL.
NEXT SLIDE.

BEW-HA-HA!
BEW-HA-HA!!

WE HAVE TWO MORE CHARACTERS. WHAT DO WE LEARN FROM THIS SECOND CHARACTER-FOCUSED PANEL?
BEW-HA-HA!
BEW-HA-
WE'VE GOT SOME HEROES TO COUNTER THE VILLAIN.
SUPERHERO WIENER DOGS. WHO DOESN'T LIKE THAT?

READER, WHAT DO YOU THINK ABOUT THESE TWO NEW CHARACTERS?
I KNOW, RIGHT?

WITH OUR CHARACTERS BETTER UNDERSTOOD, LET'S ADD A ***CONFLICT PANEL***. A CONFLICT PANEL FOCUSES ON THE PRIMARY ***TENSION(S)*** BEHIND THE STORY.

HERE ARE THREE *RISING ACTION* PANELS.

OKAY, READER, SO OBVIOUSLY THE LEAGUE IS GOING TO SAY THAT THE SETTING IS IN AN *OFFICE* OF SOME SORT. BUT YOU AND I KNOW A BIT *MORE*, DON'T WE?

OKAY, WITH OUR PLOT, CHARACTERS, RISING ACTION, CONFLICT, AND SETTING PANELS ALL IN PLACE, OUR STORY NEEDS TO COME TO SOME SORT OF *CLIMAX*.

A *CLIMAX PANEL* BRINGS ALL THE *RISING ACTION*, ALL THE INTENSITY IN A STORY, TO A *POINT*.
WHEN WE LEFT OUR STORY, DR. VICIOUS HAD AIMED HER *MIND-CONTROL GOGGLES* AT MR. MAX HANDSOME, WHO, IN RESPONSE, IS USING HIS *SUPER BOA* TO OVERPOWER DR.VICIOUS' MIND-CONTROL GOGGLES BEAM.

OKAY, NOW FOR A CLIMAX PANEL...
KA-POW!

A BATTLE BETWEEN GOOD AND EVIL MAKES FOR A GOOD CLIMAX TO OUR STORY, RIGHT? BUT AFTER SUCH A CLIMAX, HOW DOES THE STORY RESOLVE ITSELF?
KA-POW!
THE NEXT FEW RESOLUTION PANELS WILL SETTLE, OR RESOLVE, THE CONFLICT IN THIS STORY.
FINAL SLIDES, PLEASE.

NOOOO!
MR. MAX HANDSOME, I AM YOUR--

!

WHA - REALLY? WHAT HAPPENED?
YOU'RE SUPPOSED TO BARK WHEN SOMETHING HAPPENS. YOU BARK WHEN YOU SEE A FLY, A SPIDER, A BARELY-VISIBLE DUST BUNNY! AND NOT THIS?
HA! SHE BELIEVES I AM INNOCENT. DIDN'T EVEN NEED MIND-CONTROL GOGGLES.
BEW-HA-HA-HA-HA!

SO, IN WHAT WAYS ARE THESE FINAL PANELS RESOLUTION PANELS?

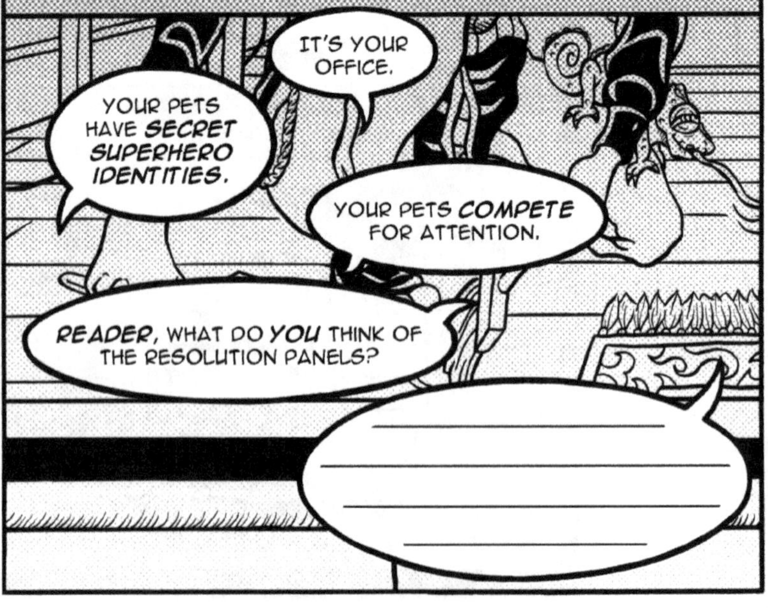
IT'S YOUR OFFICE.
YOUR PETS HAVE SECRET SUPERHERO IDENTITIES.
YOUR PETS COMPETE FOR ATTENTION.
READER, WHAT DO YOU THINK OF THE RESOLUTION PANELS?

OKAY, ONLY FOUR MORE PANEL TYPES LEFT. AND, AS I TELL TEACHERS AND LIBRARIANS, EACH OF THEM CAN BE FOUND DURING AND/OR AFTER READING A GRAPHIC NOVEL STORY; IN FACT, WE'VE ALREADY SEEN THESE FOUR TYPES OF PANELS IN OUR STORY, THUS MAKING THEM COMBINATION PANELS, PANELS THAT CONTAIN TWO OR MORE ELEMENTS OF STORY. WE JUST NEED TO GO BACK AND LOOK AGAIN.

A FORESHADOWING PANEL HINTS AT OR ALLUDES TO WHAT IS GOING TO HAPPEN IN THE STORY.

REMEMBER THIS PANEL?
ONE BEAM FROM MY MIND-CONTROL VISION AND I WILL BE THE FAVORITE, SUPER SAM. SHE WILL LOVE ME AND PUT YOU TWO IN A GLASS JAIL OF SOME KIND, WHERE I CAN TAUNT YOU. BEW-HA-HA! THE TABLES WILL TURN, THE...
SUPER SAM. SUPER SAM. SUPER SAM. DO YOU NOT FEAR MR. MAX HANDSOME?
DO I HEAR A VOLUNTEER, MR. MAX HANDSOME?

HOW IS THIS PANEL, THAT WE EARLIER LABELED A RISING ACTION PANEL, ALSO A FORE-SHADOWING PANEL?
OKAY, YOU FIRST, READER!
YES! WHAT ELSE?
IT FORESHADOWS THAT MR. MAX HANDSOME AND DR. VICIOUS WILL DO BATTLE.
DR. VICIOUS HINTS THAT THERE MAY BE AN OVERTURN OF POWER.

AND WHAT ABOUT THEME PANELS, TOO - PANELS THAT GET AT THE MAIN IDEA? WE'VE ACTUALLY SEEN ONE OF THOSE ALREADY AS WELL BUT AS A CONFLICT PANEL.
YOU WILL NEVER SUCCEED, EVIL-DOER! WE WILL NEVER LET YOU--
OH, I WILL BE GREATER THAN THE TWO OF YOU. I WILL NO LONGER BE SEEN AS 'THE CRANKY CHAMELEON.' I WILL RULE THE WORLD!
YOU NEVER...
HUUUUM!
...WIN, DR. VICIOUS.
DELUSIONAL! OUR WORLD IS BASICALLY THIS OFFICE. MOM SPENDS MOST OF HER TIME IN HERE.

WHAT THEMES DO YOU SEE?
READER?
GOOD AND EVIL.
IDENTITY.
EXCELLENT! ALL OF THESE THEMES ARE THERE, OVERLAPPING IN THIS RISING ACTION PANEL.

ONLY ONE MORE TYPE OF PANEL: SYMBOL PANELS.
A SYMBOL PANEL PRESENTS READERS WITH IMAGES OR WORDS THAT STAND FOR SOMETHING GREATER THAN THEMSELVES.

ONE BEAM FROM MY MIND-CONTROL VISION AND I WILL BE THE FAVORITE, SUPER SAM. SHE WILL LOVE ME AND PUT YOU TWO IN A GLASS JAIL OF SOME KIND, WHERE I CAN TAUNT YOU. BEW-HA-HA! THE TABLES WILL TURN, THE
SUPER SAM. SUPER SAM. SUPER SAM. DO YOU NOT FEAR MR. MAX HANDSOME?
DO I HEAR A VOLUNTEER, MR. MAX HANDSOME?
YOU WILL NEVER SUCCEED, EVIL-DOER! WE WILL NEVER LET YOU--
OH, I WILL BE GREATER THAN THE TWO OF YOU. I WILL NO LONGER BE SEEN AS 'THE CRANKY CHAMELEON.' I WILL RULE THE WORLD!
YOU NEVER...
HUUUUM!
...WIN, DR. VICIOUS.
DELUSIONAL! OUR WORLD IS BASICALLY THIS OFFICE. MOM SPENDS MOST OF HER TIME IN HERE.
JUST ONE LAST TIME, THINK ABOUT OUR LAST TWO SLIDES. DO YOU SEE ANY SYMBOLS IN THOSE PANELS?
READER?
THE COSTUMES SYMBOLIZE DIFFERENT POWERS.
MR. MAX HANDSOME'S BOA MAKES HIM LOOK LAID BACK BUT LIKE A SHOW-OFF, TOO. SUPER SAM'S COSTUME IS SERIOUS, SYMBOLIC OF A TRADITIONAL SUPERHERO.
HEY, RACHEL, BEFORE WE LEAVE THIS CHAPTER, DO YOU THINK YOU COULD GIVE OUR READERS A COOL, VISUAL RECAP OF THE DIFFERENT TYPES OF GRAPHIC NOVEL PANELS?
SURE THING, KATIE.

READER, BEFORE WE MOVE ON TO CHAPTER 4, RACHEL AND I WANT TO MAKE SURE YOU FEEL COMFORTABLE WITH THE ***VARIOUS TYPES*** OF GRAPHIC NOVEL PANELS AND HOW THEY RELATE TO ***TRADITIONAL ELEMENTS*** OF STORY. SO, RACHEL IS GOING TO PRESENT YOU WITH A FUN OPPORTUNITY TO NOT ONLY REFLECT ON THESE ***TERMS*** AND THEIR CORRESPONDING ***DEFINITIONS***, BUT ALSO TO ADD YOUR OWN ILLUSTRATIONS. AFTER EACH TERM AND ITS DEFINITION, PLEASE THINK BACK ON OUR STORY, AND USE ***WORDS*** OR ***IMAGES*** TO BRING THE TERM AND ITS DEFINITION TOGETHER WITH AN EXAMPLE FROM OUR STORY.

3. SETTING PANELS
focus on the location(s) where the story takes place
4. RISING ACTION PANELS
develop the set of events that increase the tension or conflict in the story
7. RESOLUTION PANELS
follow the climax and resolve the tension in the story
8. FORESHADOWING PANELS
hint at future events to come in the story
11. COMBINATION STORY PANELS
combine two or more of the above listed panels
ONCE TEACHERS UNDERSTAND HOW GRAPHIC NOVEL PANELS *COMPLEMENT* TEACHING TRADITIONAL ELEMENTS OF STORY, THEY ARE NEXT READY TO LEARN THE TERM "*GUTTER*."
I ALWAYS LIKE TO EXPLAIN GUTTERS TO TEACHERS BY SAYING...

RECORD YOUR
THOUGHTS

*MAKING COMICS: STORYTELLING SECRETS OF COMICS, MANGA AND GRAPHIC NOVELS. NEW YORK, NY: HARPERCOLLINS.

MCCLOUD IDENTIFIES THE SIX TYPES OF GUTTERS AS...
1. MOMENT-TO-MOMENT GUTTER – From one panel to the next, readers witness little closure and simply see something in the storyline from one instance to the next instance.
2. SCENE-TO-SCENE GUTTER – From one panel to the next, readers move from setting to setting.
3. SUBJECT-TO-SUBJECT GUTTER – In these gutter spaces, readers move from an initial panel focused on one or more characters or a subject to the next panel focused on another character or subject.
4. ACTION-TO-ACTION GUTTER – From one panel to the next, readers find the pace of the story increases and see a subject going through a series of quick, active transitions.
5. ASPECT-TO-ASPECT GUTTER – Similar to tone or mood, the transition between these panels focuses on the feelings or emotions being conveyed in the storyline.
6. NON-SEQUITER GUTTER – Although the transition between these panels may at first seem nonsensical, there is indeed a deeper, often thematic, foreshadowed, or symbolic meaning behind them.

MCCLOUD'S IDENTIFICATION OF THE SIX TYPES OF GRAPHIC NOVEL GUTTERS IS VERY WELL RESPECTED. YET, I HAVE HAD SOME STUDENTS SUGGEST THAT WE ADD A ***SEVENTH GUTTER***. SOME STUDENTS HAVE FELT AS THOUGH GRAPHIC NOVEL GUTTERS CAN ALSO BE ***DUALISTIC*** IN NATURE, SIMILAR TO THE ***COMBINATION STORY PANEL***.

LET'S LOOK AT AN ***EXAMPLE***...

BECAUSE THESE TWO PANELS SHOW DR. VICIOUS FROM ***ONE INSTANCE*** OR MOMENT TO THE ***NEXT***, THE GUTTER BETWEEN THEM IS MOST LIKELY A ***MOMENT-TO-MOMENT GUTTER***.

BUT EVEN THOUGH THIS IS CLEARLY A ***MOMENT-TO-MOMENT GUTTER***, IT CAN ALSO, DUE TO ITS CONVEYANCE OF DR. VICIOUS' SINISTER MOOD, BE AN ***ASPECT-TO-ASPECT GUTTER*** THAT REFLECTS HER MOOD.

The Seven Types of Graphic Novel Gutters
The reader-friendly spaces in between panels where readers transform two or more ideas into a seamless whole.
MCCLOUD'S SIX TYPES OF GUTTERS
1. MOMENT-TO-MOMENT GUTTER – From one panel to the next, readers witness little closure and simply see something in the storyline from one instance to the next instance.
2. SCENE-TO-SCENE GUTTER – From one panel to the next, readers move from setting to setting.
3. SUBJECT-TO-SUBJECT GUTTER – In these gutter spaces, readers move from an initial panel focused on one or more characters or a subject to the next panel focused on another character or subject.
4. ACTION-TO-ACTION GUTTER – From one panel to the next, readers find the pace of the story increases and see a subject going through a series of quick, active transitions.
5. ASPECT-TO-ASPECT GUTTER – Similar to tone or mood, the transition between these panels focuses on the feelings or emotions being conveyed in the storyline.
6. NON-SEQUITER GUTTER – Although the transition between these panels may at first seem nonsensical, there is indeed a deeper, often thematic, foreshadowed, or symbolic meaning behind them.
And Introducing a Seventh Type of Graphic Novel Gutter…
7. **COMBINATION GUTTER –** A gutter combining two or more of McCloud's (1993) original six types of gutters.

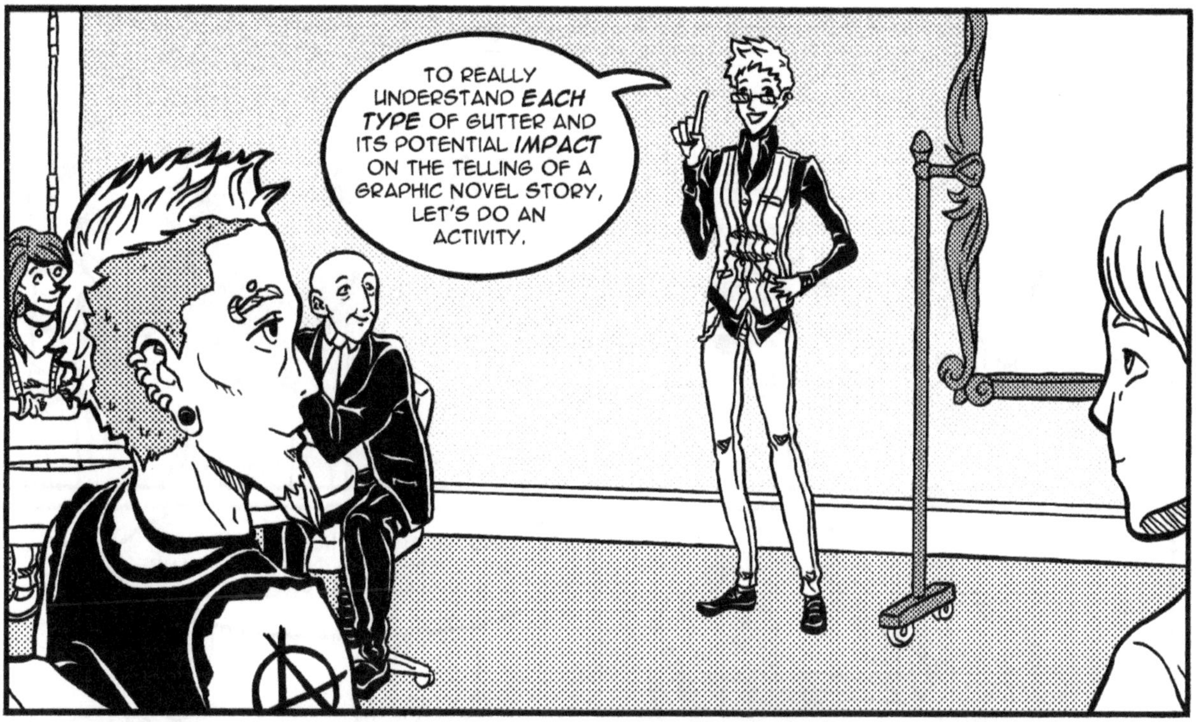

1. In your table groups, review McCloud's six types of gutters. Review the added seventh gutter as well.

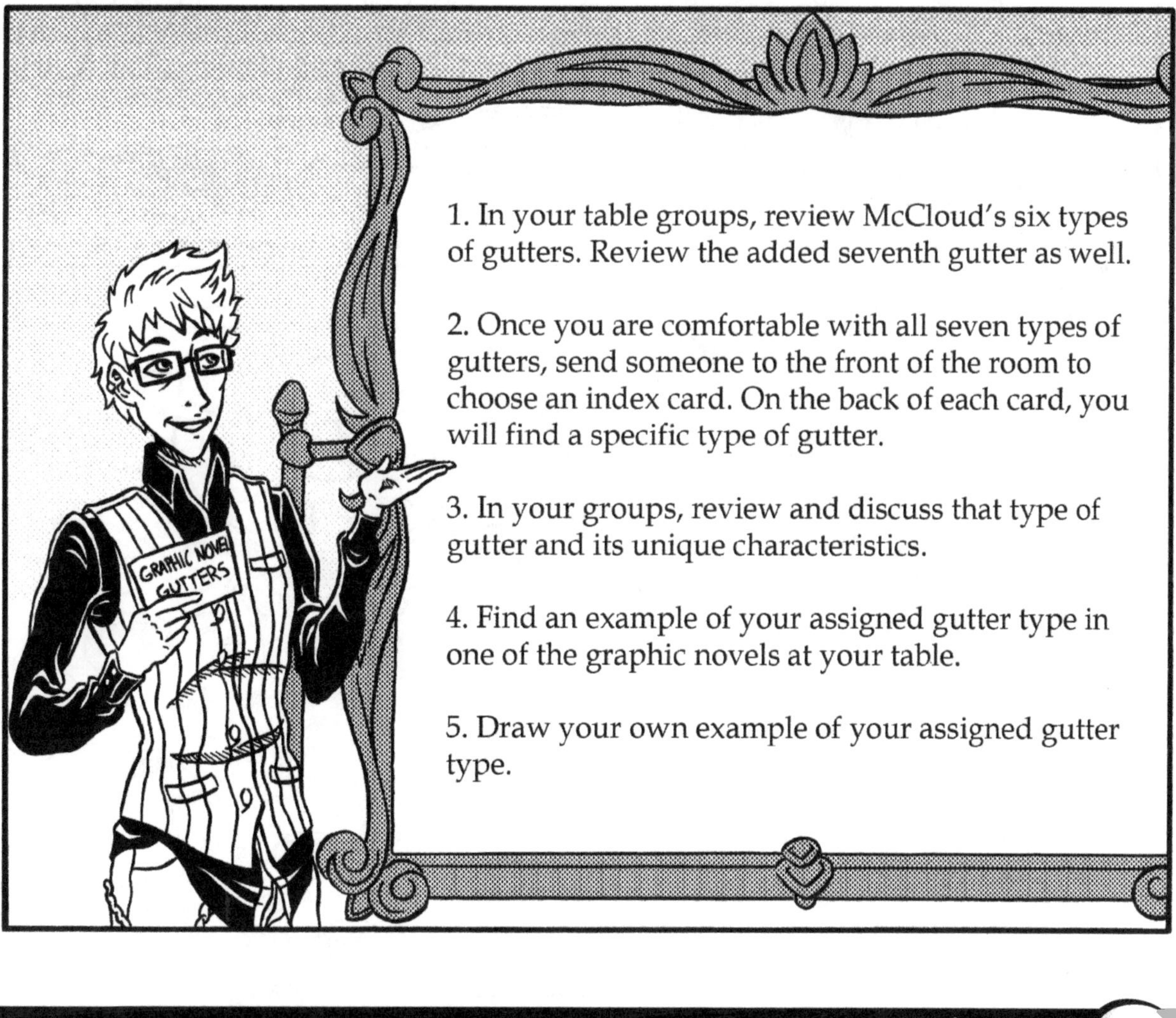

2. Once you are comfortable with all seven types of gutters, send someone to the front of the room to choose an index card. On the back of each card, you will find a specific type of gutter.

3. In your groups, review and discuss that type of gutter and its unique characteristics.

4. Find an example of your assigned gutter type in one of the graphic novels at your table.

5. Draw your own example of your assigned gutter type.

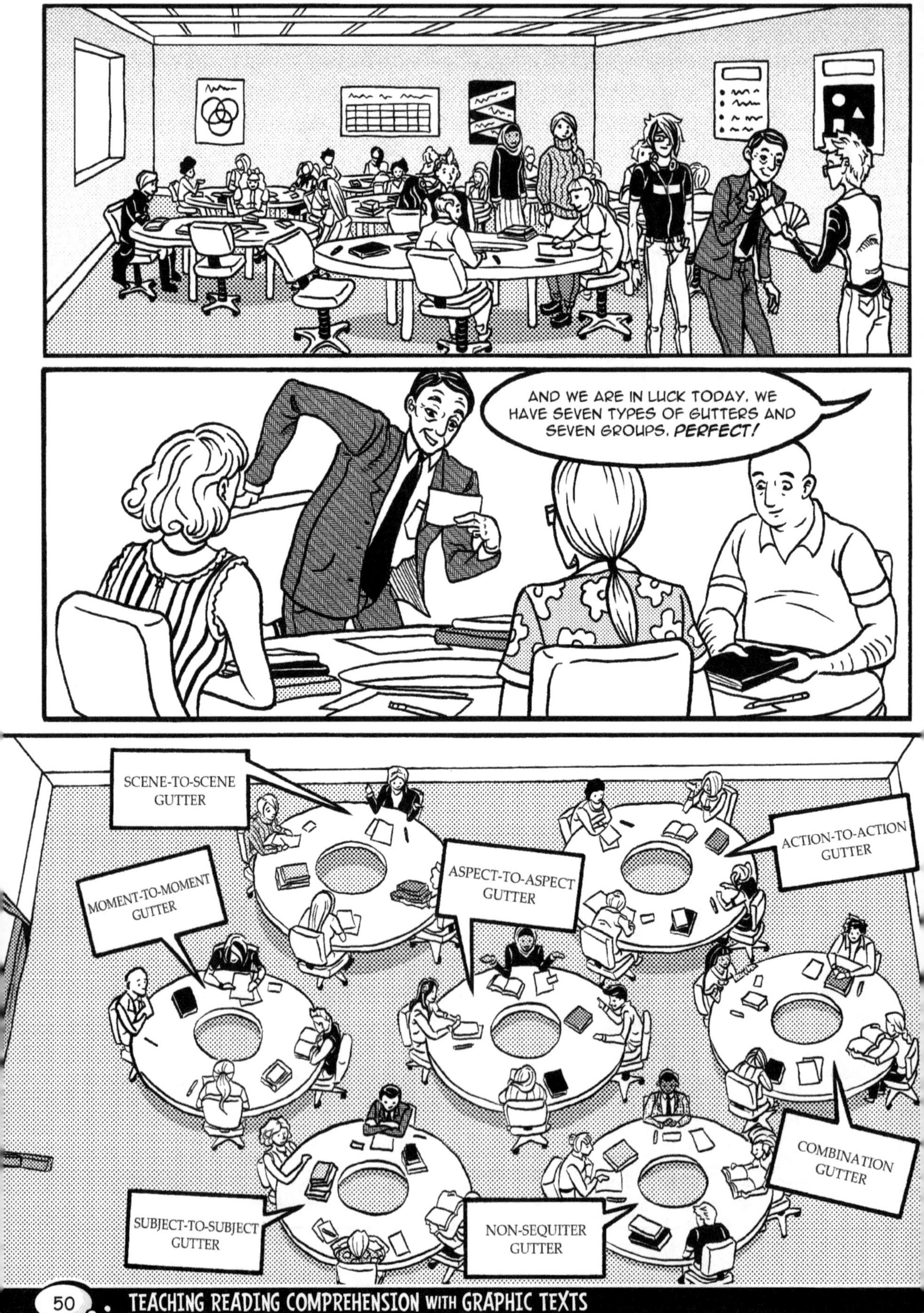

SCENE-TO-SCENE GUTTER
ACTION-TO-ACTION GUTTER
MOMENT-TO-MOMENT GUTTER
ASPECT-TO-ASPECT GUTTER
COMBINATION GUTTER
SUBJECT-TO-SUBJECT GUTTER
NON-SEQUITER GUTTER

SO WE HAVE **SUBJECT-TO-SUBJECT**. WANNA FIND SOME GOOD **EXAMPLES** FIRST?

U.S.
CONSTITUTION

OKAY, ONE GROUP AT A TIME, LET'S SEE WHAT YOU DISCOVERED. YOU CAN USE THE DOCUMENT CAMERA TO DISPLAY YOUR ***CARD***, YOUR ***GRAPHIC NOVEL EXAMPLE***, AND, MOST EXCITINGLY, YOUR GROUP'S ***OWN EXAMPLE***. LET'S START WITH THE ***MOMENT-TO-MOMENT*** GUTTER GROUP.

MOMENT-TO-MOMENT GUTTER
From one panel to the next, readers witness little closure and simply see something in the story from one instance to the next instance.

OUR GROUP THOUGHT PAGE 7 OF ***TELGEMEIER'S SMILE*** HAD A GREAT ***MOMENT-TO-MOMENT*** GUTTER SEQUENCE. FROM ONE MOMENT TO THE NEXT, THE READER SEES RAINA AS SHE EXPERIENCES HER TRIP, FALL, INJURY, AND INITIAL REACTIONS.

...

HANDS... LEGS...

NOTHING BROKEN.

YOU KNOW THE SECONDS OR MOMENTS WHEN YOUR CELL PHONE STARTS TO RING, AND IT'S ***TOTALLY*** THE WRONG TIME TO ANSWER IT? THAT'S A TOTAL MOMENT-TO-MOMENT GUTTER EXPERIENCE. YOU DO YOUR BEST TO MAKE IT STOP RINGING AS ***EACH MOMENT PASSES***.

RIING
RING
RING
!

RING
RING
RING

SWEET EXAMPLE! HOW MANY OF YOU, AND I INCLUDE ***MYSELF*** IN THAT CATEGORY, HAVE TO REMIND YOURSELVES TO TURN OFF YOUR CELL PHONES WHEN YOU GO INTO A QUIET PLACE?
OK, ***SCENE-TO-SCENE*** GROUP, YOU'RE UP.

SCENE-TO-SCENE GUTTER
From one panel to the next, readers move from setting to setting.
OUR GROUP FOUND A REALLY COOL ***SCENE-TO-SCENE*** GUTTER TRANSITION IN A NONFICTION GRAPHIC NOVEL BY C. M. BUTZER. YOU SHOULD LOOK IT UP. THE TITLE IS ***GETTYSBURG: THE GRAPHIC NOVEL.***
SO, WE FOUND IT COOL WHEN...

WE THOUGHT THESE PAGES REALLY ILLUSTRATED THE ***SCENE-BY-SCENE*** ARRIVAL OF PRESIDENT LINCOLN AT GETTYSBURG, THE DAY BEFORE HIS FAMOUS GETTYSBURG ADDRESS.

GETTYSBURG STATION

WELCOME

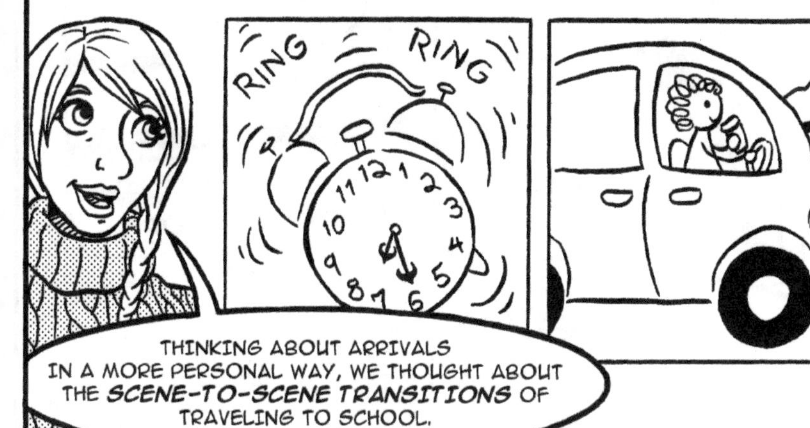
RING RING
THINKING ABOUT ARRIVALS IN A MORE PERSONAL WAY, WE THOUGHT ABOUT THE ***SCENE-TO-SCENE TRANSITIONS*** OF TRAVELING TO SCHOOL.

ON THE SECOND PAGE OF BEN HATKE'S ***ZITA THE SPACEGIRL***, THE READER COMES ACROSS A ***SUBJECT-TO-SUBJECT*** GUTTER BETWEEN AN INITIAL PANEL SHOWING ZITA AS THE CHARACTER AND THE FOLLOWING PANEL SHOWING JOSEPH AS THE CHARACTER.

SUBJECT-TO-SUBJECT GUTTERS CARRY A LOT OF WEIGHT IN ORDER TO ***PROGRESS THE STORY***. THIS MADE OUR GROUP THINK OF ALL THE PLANNING AND VARIOUS SUBJECTS INVOLVED IN A SCHOOL FIELD TRIP. THERE ARE SO MANY ***SUBJECT-FOCUSED MOMENTS*** THAT OCCUR DURING A FIELD TRIP, ESPECIALLY AS TEACHERS AND STUDENTS GET READY IN THE MORNING.

SCHOOL FIELD TRIPS ARE CERTAINLY SUBJECT-TO-SUBJECT DAYS. THEY ARE DAYS FULL OF ***SNAPSHOTS***, ***SUBJECT-TO-SUBJECT*** OPPORTUNITIES.
WHERE IS OUR ***ACTION-TO-ACTION*** GUTTER GROUP?

ACTION-TO-ACTION GUTTERS ARE FUN. IN AN ACTION-TO-ACTION GUTTER, THE ***PACE*** OF THE STORY INCREASES AND A SINGLE SUBJECT GOES THROUGH A SERIES OF ***QUICK TRANSITIONS***.

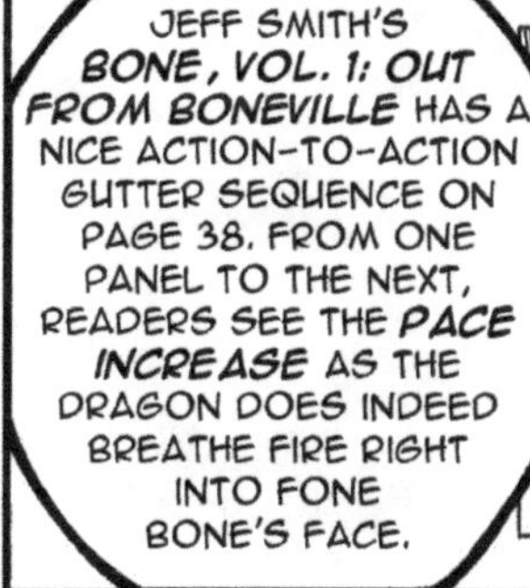
JEFF SMITH'S ***BONE, VOL. 1: OUT FROM BONEVILLE*** HAS A NICE ACTION-TO-ACTION GUTTER SEQUENCE ON PAGE 38. FROM ONE PANEL TO THE NEXT, READERS SEE THE ***PACE INCREASE*** AS THE DRAGON DOES INDEED BREATHE FIRE RIGHT INTO FONE BONE'S FACE.

WHAT'S TH' MATTER? CAN'T YOU BREATHE FIRE?

FOOMP

UM.
THAT'S RIGHT, KID. NEVER PLAY AN ACE IF A TWO WILL DO.

WHAT ELSE CAN WE SAY? A ***SWORD FIGHT***: A CLASSIC ACTION-TO-ACTION SEQUENCE.

OUR GROUP TALKED ABOUT FEELING LIKE THIS POOR GUY AT ONE POINT OR ANOTHER. WHEN THE TEACHER IS NOT PLEASED WITH THE TEST GRADES AND IS RETURNING TESTS TO STUDENTS, THE WHOLE CLASS GETS **NERVOUS**. THE TEACHER'S MOOD AFFECTS THE STUDENTS' MOODS. YET WHEN WE FIND OUT THAT WE ARE ONE OF THE SEEMINGLY SMALL NUMBER OF STUDENTS WHO DID WELL, OUR **MOOD** CAN **DRASTICALLY CHANGE**.

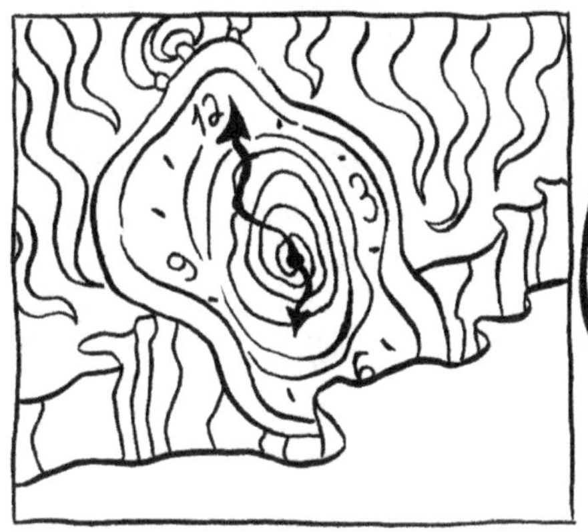

OUR GROUP FELT LIKE WE ARE SOMETIMES AT OUR MOST NONSENSICAL WHEN WE LOSE OUR SENSE OF CONTROL. IT REMINDED US OF BEING STUCK IN TRAFFIC.

THIS GUTTER SEQUENCE SEEMS EASY TO LABEL. IT'S FOCUSED ON ***ONE SUBJECT*** TO THE ***NEXT***. AT THE END OF THE FOUR-PANEL SEQUENCE, A NEW SUBJECT (THE BEAR) TURNS THE SUBJECT FOCUS ON ITS HEAD AND ADDS A NERVOUS, FRANTIC, AND EMOTIONAL TONE TO THE FOUR-PANEL SEQUENCE; IT'S NOW AN ***ASPECT-TO-ASPECT*** GUTTER SEQUENCE AS WELL.

MOMENT-TO-MOMENT

FROM ONE PANEL TO THE NEXT, READERS WITNESS LITTLE CLOSURE AND SIMPLY SEE SOMETHING IN THE STORYLINE FROM ONE INSTANCE TO THE NEXT INSTANCE.

SCENE-TO-SCENE

FROM ONE PANEL TO THE NEXT, READERS MOVE FROM SETTING TO SETTING.

SUBJECT-TO-SUBJECT

IN THESE GUTTER SPACES, READERS MOVE FROM AN INITIAL PANEL FOCUSED ON ONE OR MORE CHARACTERS OR A SUBJECT TO THE NEXT PANEL FOCUSED ON ANOTHER CHARACTER OR SUBJECT.

ACTION-TO-ACTION

FROM ONE PANEL TO THE NEXT, READERS FIND THE PACE OF THE STORY INCREASES AND SEE A SUBJECT GOING THROUGH A SERIES OF QUICK, ACTIVE TRANSITIONS.

ASPECT-TO-ASPECT

SIMILAR TO TONE OR MOOD, THE TRANSITION BETWEEN THESE PANELS FOCUSES ON THE FEELINGS OR EMOTIONS BEING CONVEYED IN THE STORYLINE.

NON-SEQUITUR

ALTHOUGH THE TRANSITION BETWEEN THESE PANELS MAY AT FIRST SEEM NONSENSICAL, THERE IS INDEED A DEEPER, OFTEN THEMATIC, FORESHADOWED, OR SYMBOLIC MEANING BEHIND THEM.

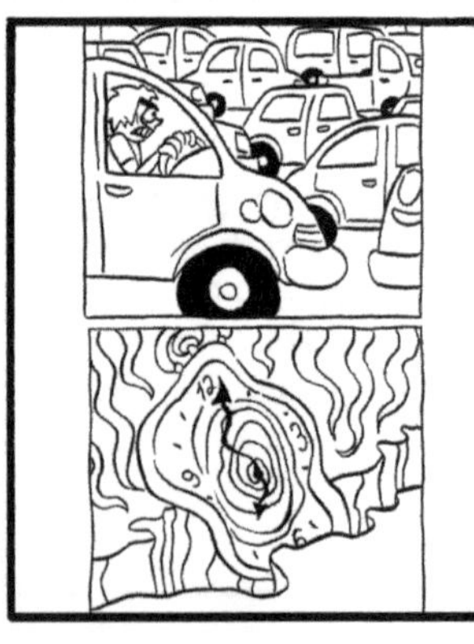

COMBINATION

A GUTTER COMBINING TWO OR MORE OF MCCLOUD'S ORIGINAL SIX TYPES OF GUTTERS.

RECORD YOUR THOUGHTS

OK, SO WE ARE ABOUT OUT OF TIME FOR TODAY. ANYONE HAVE ANY QUESTIONS, COMMENTS, CONCERNS, DILEMMAS, PARANOIAS, PHOBIAS, OR BITTER COMPLAINTS?

WHAT ARE THE ***BUBBLE THINGS?***

BALLOONS! A WHOLE NEW CHAPTER FOR ANOTHER DAY.

I WON'T LOOK AT COMICS AND GRAPHIC NOVELS THE SAME WAY AGAIN.

I KNOW, RIGHT?

SEE YOU NEXT WEEK!

BYE!

SEE YA LATER, EVERYONE.

NEXT WEEK'S TOPIC: TEACHING ***READING COMPREHENSION*** WITH GRAPHIC NOVEL ***BALLOONS***. FUN....

MAY
JUNE
JULY
AUGUST
EMBER

OKAY, TIME FOR GRAPHIC NOVEL BALLOONS...
ONE YEAR LATER...
WHEN I FIRST LEARNED WHAT IT MEANT TO READ GRAPHIC NOVELS, MY TEACHER TALKED TO US ABOUT THE ***THREE*** MOST COMMON ***TYPES OF GRAPHIC NOVEL BALLOONS.***
BEFORE WE DO THAT THOUGH, LET'S LOOK AT AN ***OVERALL DEFINITION*** OF BALLOONS. ON THE TOP OF YOUR HANDOUTS, YOU CAN FIND THAT DEFINITION.
LET'S LOOK AT AN ***EXAMPLE.***
Graphic Novel Balloons...
Are usually found inside a panel and create a visual boundary that typically contains textual elements or indicators critical to the story.
Graphic Novel Balloons:

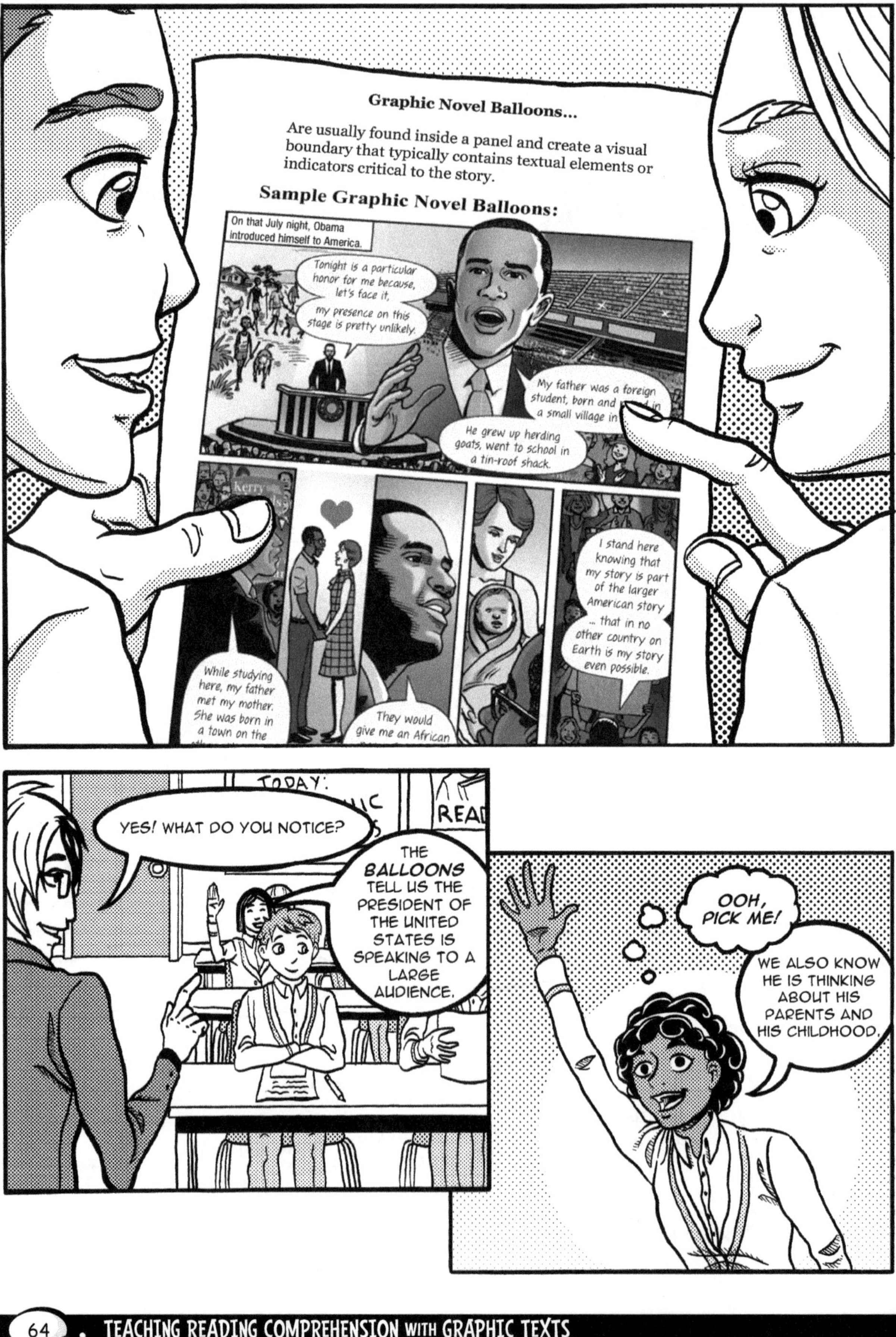

Graphic Novel Balloons...

Are usually found inside a panel and create a visual boundary that typically contains textual elements or indicators critical to the story.

Sample Graphic Novel Balloons:

On that July night, Obama introduced himself to America.

Tonight is a particular honor for me because, let's face it,

my presence on this stage is pretty unlikely.

My father was a foreign student, born and ... in a small village in

He grew up herding goats, went to school in a tin-roof shack.

While studying here, my father met my mother. She was born in a town on the

They would give me an African

I stand here knowing that my story is part of the larger American story

... that in no other country on Earth is my story even possible.

IF I DIDN'T SEE BALLOONS, I WOULDN'T KNOW HE WAS SPEAKING.
BALLOONS USE WORDS TO SORTA HELP PICTURES TELL A STORY.
IF I WERE IN A GRAPHIC NOVEL RIGHT NOW, THERE WOULD BE A BALLOON ABOVE MY HEAD SAYING WHAT I AM SAYING RIGHT NOW. CAN'T YOU JUST SEE IT?
YEAH, BUT WHO WANTS TO HEAR WHAT YOU HAVE TO SAY?
NI-CE! TEAM WORK!
BALLOONS ARE LIKE MOVIE SUBTITLES.
YEAH, I CAN READ THEM WHENEVER I NEED 'EM.
YOU CAN GO BACK TO THEM TOO, LIKE A REFERENCE OR TO RE-READ IF YOU DON'T GET IT.
READ

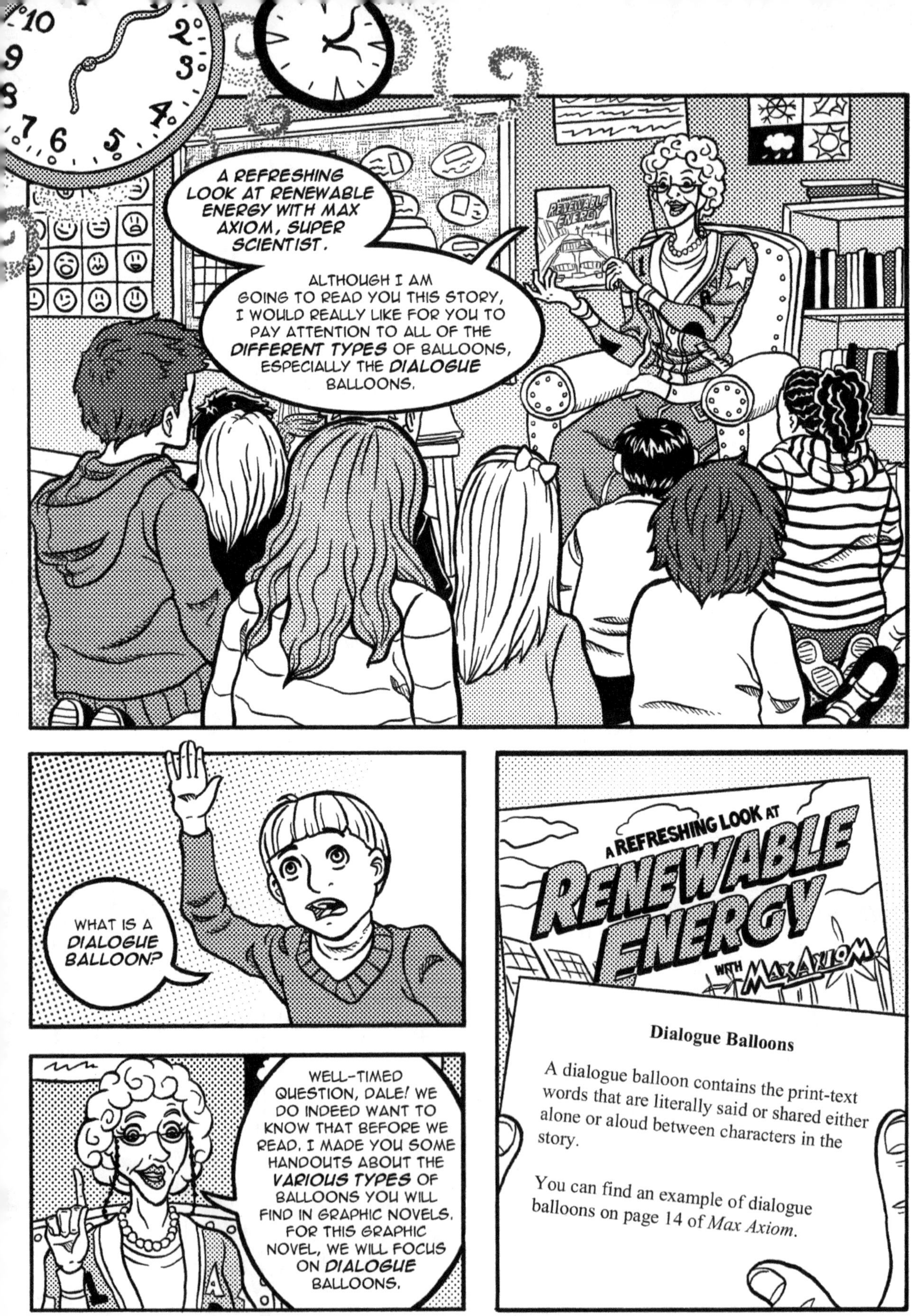

A REFRESHING LOOK AT RENEWABLE ENERGY WITH MAX AXIOM, SUPER SCIENTIST.

ALTHOUGH I AM GOING TO READ YOU THIS STORY, I WOULD REALLY LIKE FOR YOU TO PAY ATTENTION TO ALL OF THE ***DIFFERENT TYPES*** OF BALLOONS, ESPECIALLY THE ***DIALOGUE*** BALLOONS.

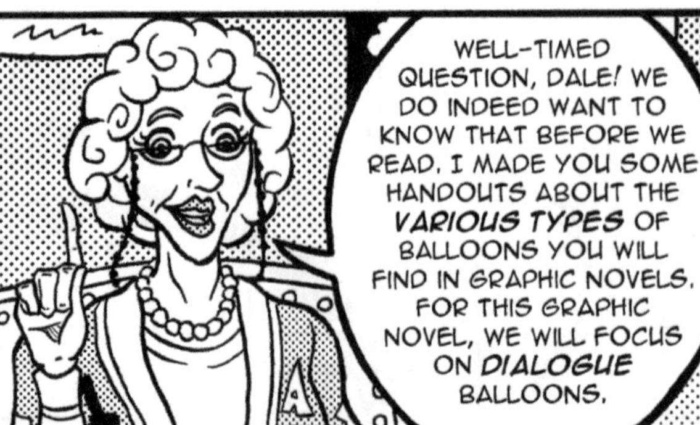

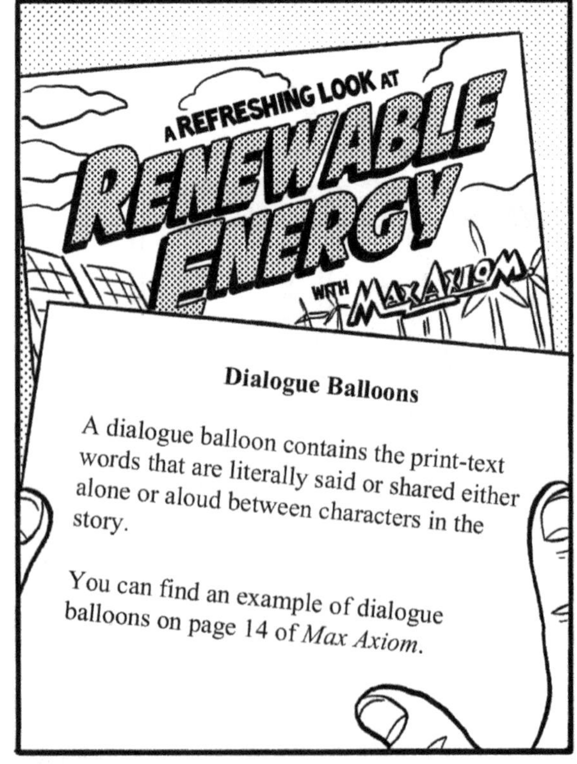

Dialogue Balloons

A dialogue balloon contains the print-text words that are literally said or shared either alone or aloud between characters in the story.

You can find an example of dialogue balloons on page 14 of *Max Axiom*.

SECTION 3 LARGE-SCALE RENEWABLE ENERGY
The sun isn't our only renewable energy source. The Grand Coulee Dam in Washington State uses moving water to create power.
WOOOOOSSH!
Thanks, Carlos. Would you give me a tour of the power plant?
Follow me. I'll show you how we create electricity with waterpower.
The water from the Columbia River fills a deep reservoir.
Tunnels at the bottom of the dam channel water to the turbines.
RESERVOIR
TURBINES
14

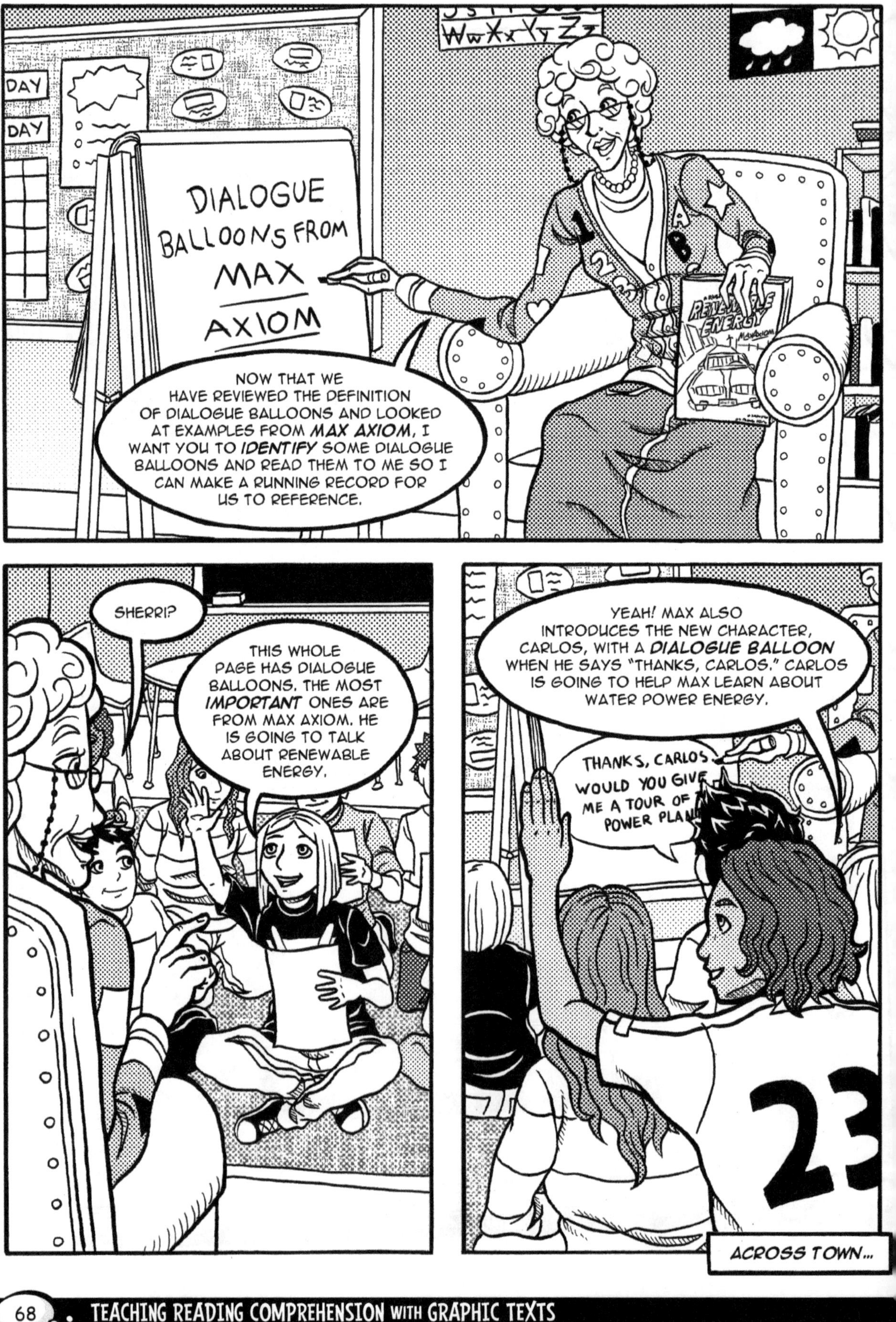

DIALOGUE BALLOONS FROM MAX AXIOM

NOW THAT WE HAVE REVIEWED THE DEFINITION OF DIALOGUE BALLOONS AND LOOKED AT EXAMPLES FROM ***MAX AXIOM***, I WANT YOU TO ***IDENTIFY*** SOME DIALOGUE BALLOONS AND READ THEM TO ME SO I CAN MAKE A RUNNING RECORD FOR US TO REFERENCE.

OKAY, NOW THAT WE KNOW DIALOGUE BALLOONS, LET'S SPEND SOME TIME ON THOUGHT BALLOONS...
RIIING
RING
HA! METACOGNITION FIRST THING IN THE MORNING! THINKING ABOUT MY THINKING! IT'S LIKE I CAN SEE MY OWN THOUGHT BALLOONS!
WELCOME TO DAY TWO OF GRAPHIC NOVEL BALLOONS!
THOUGHT BALLOONS
MS. ROSE
I WONDER IF I EVER HAVE THOUGHT BALLOONS?
DIALOGUE BALLOONS = CHARACTERS TALKING TO EACH OTHER.

TO DAY TWO OF
VEL BALLOONS!
IT BALLOONS
THOUGHT BALLOONS ARE PRETTY COOL AND VERY REVEALING. THEY FOCUS ON A CHARACTER'S SECRET AND PRIVATE THOUGHTS. IN A WAY, THEY GIVE GRAPHIC NOVEL READERS INSIDER TIPS. THESE TIPS ARE CLUES TO WHAT THE CHARACTER ACTUALLY THINKS, IN IMAGES AND/OR WORDS, BUT MAY NOT SAY OUT LOUD.

LET'S DO AN ACTIVITY TO HELP US BETTER UNDERSTAND THOUGHT BALLOONS. FOR JUST A FEW MINUTES, LET'S CLOSE OUR EYES AND THINK ABOUT OUR FAVORITE THING IN THE WORLD.
THOUGHT BALLOONS

WITH YOUR EYES STILL CLOSED, RAISE YOUR HAND WHEN YOU ARE READY TO SHARE YOUR THOUGHT BALLOON....

PLEASE LET ME SEE SOME HANDS RAISED!

FINAL EXAM
A++++
GO TEAM!
15
ACTION
OH MAN! GOING TO...FALL ASLEEP. WHAT WAS THE QUESTION?
LUNCH. WHAT TIME IS LUNCH?
ZOOM
WHAT IF I OPEN MY EYES? SOMEONE ELSE PROBABLY HAS THEIR EYES OPEN.
ZOO
WELCOME!
YUM, NOM-NOM-NOM. MEXICAN FOOD!
22

LATER...

Thought balloons:

Insider tips or clues about what a character is really thinking.

Sample page from *Sunken Wonder*.

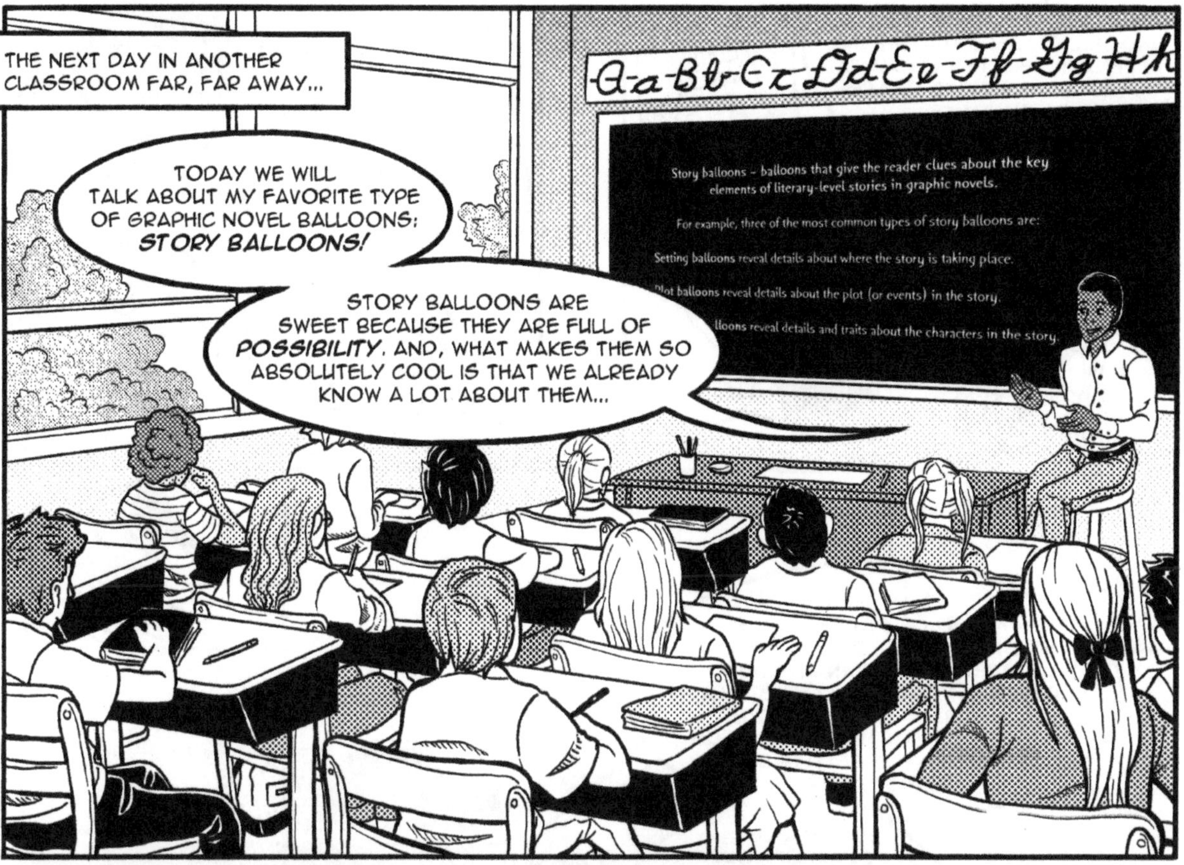

THE NEXT DAY IN ANOTHER CLASSROOM FAR, FAR AWAY...

Aa Bb Cc Dd Ee Ff Gg Hh

TODAY WE WILL TALK ABOUT MY FAVORITE TYPE OF GRAPHIC NOVEL BALLOONS: ***STORY BALLOONS!***

STORY BALLOONS ARE SWEET BECAUSE THEY ARE FULL OF ***POSSIBILITY***. AND, WHAT MAKES THEM SO ABSOLUTELY COOL IS THAT WE ALREADY KNOW A LOT ABOUT THEM...

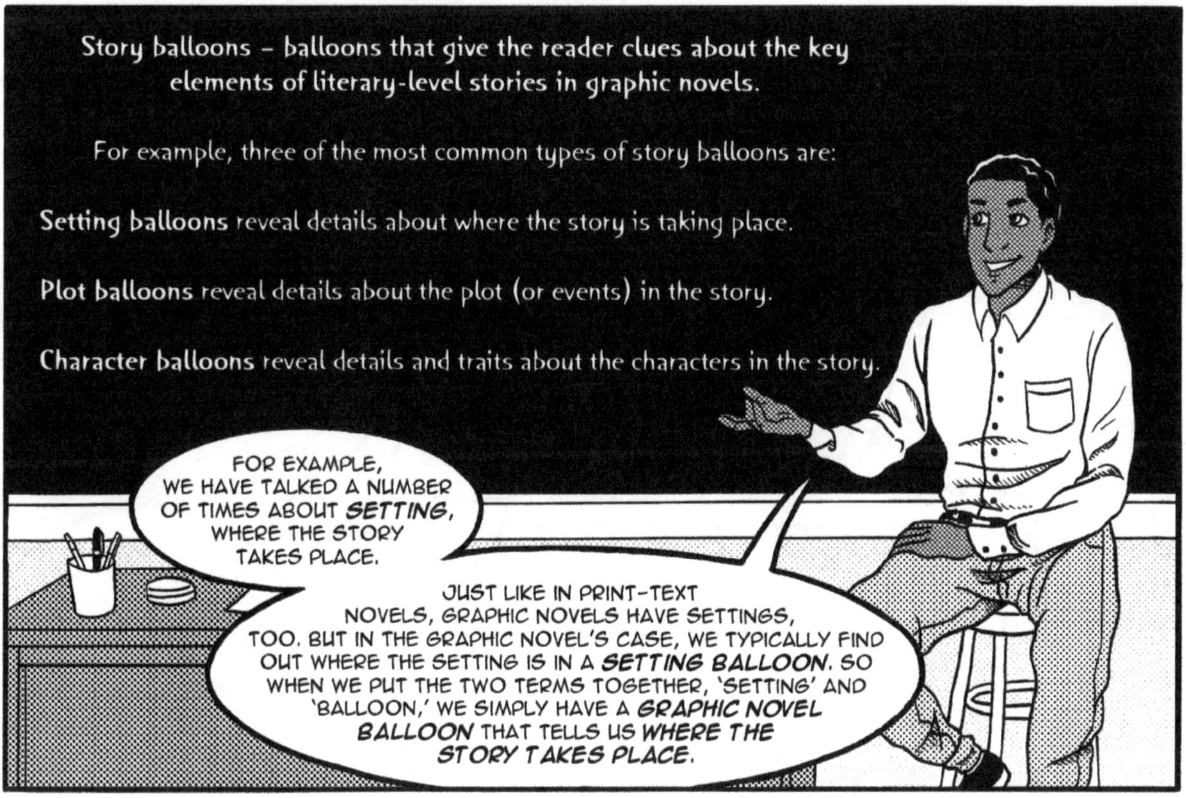

Story balloons – balloons that give the reader clues about the key elements of literary-level stories in graphic novels.

For example, three of the most common types of story balloons are:

Setting balloons reveal details about where the story is taking place.

Plot balloons reveal details about the plot (or events) in the story.

Character balloons reveal details and traits about the characters in the story.

FOR EXAMPLE, WE HAVE TALKED A NUMBER OF TIMES ABOUT ***SETTING***, WHERE THE STORY TAKES PLACE.

JUST LIKE IN PRINT-TEXT NOVELS, GRAPHIC NOVELS HAVE SETTINGS, TOO. BUT IN THE GRAPHIC NOVEL'S CASE, WE TYPICALLY FIND OUT WHERE THE SETTING IS IN A ***SETTING BALLOON***. SO WHEN WE PUT THE TWO TERMS TOGETHER, 'SETTING' AND 'BALLOON,' WE SIMPLY HAVE A ***GRAPHIC NOVEL BALLOON*** THAT TELLS US ***WHERE THE STORY TAKES PLACE***.

MY SETTING BALLOON WOULD LOOK LIKE THE LIBERTY BELL AND TELL READERS THAT WE ARE IN PHILADELPHIA, PENNSYLVANIA, WHERE I WON FIRST PLACE IN MY DANCE COMPETITION.
PHILADELPHIA
PA DANCE COMPETITION
1
HUNTER, GO AHEAD.
I AM AT THE BEACH SURFING, AND MY SETTING BALLOON IS A CLOUD IN THE SKY THAT SAYS "SAN DIEGO, CALIFORNIA."
CA
SAN DIEGO
JUNE 30, 1863. GETTYSBURG, PENNSYLVANIA.
AS WE SEE ON PAGE 10 OF GETTYSBURG: THE GRAPHIC NOVEL, THE CREATOR, C.M. BUTZER, HAS DRAWN AN AWESOME-LOOKING SETTING BALLOON. LOOKING LIKE A BANNER, THIS UNIQUE GRAPHIC NOVEL BALLOON TELLS US THE SETTING IS GETTYSBURG, PENNSYLVANIA.
THINK OF SOME OF YOUR OWN FAVORITE PLACES TO VISIT OR TO GO ON VACATION. WHEN YOU ARE READY TO SHARE, RAISE YOUR HAND AND TELL US WHAT WE WOULD SEE IN YOUR SETTING BALLOON.
I'M IN BED, SLEEPING IN ON A SNOW DAY. THE TV IN MY ROOM IS ON MUTE, BUT THE READER CAN SEE IT'S A SETTING BALLOON BECAUSE THE NEWS REPORTER HAS A TICKER BELOW HIM THAT READS "NO SCHOOL FOR POLK COUNTY."
NO SCHOOL FOR POLK COUNTY
DUDE, CLASSIC!
HAHAHA!
YOU WISH!
WE LIVE IN THE DESERT. THERE ARE NO SNOW DAYS HERE. YOUR DREAM SETTING BALLOON IS A SNOW DAY MIRACLE!
DESERT VIEW SKATE PARK
EVEN THOUGH I'M NOT SLEEPING IN FOR A SNOW DAY, WHICH WOULD BE SWEET, I SEE MYSELF ON A SKATE RAMP DOING A FLIP OFF THE RAMP I BUILT, AND MY SETTING BALLOON IS GRAFFITI ON THE SIDE OF THE SKATE PARK POOL SAYING "DESERT VIEW SKATE PARK."

ANOTHER SCHOOL DAY, ANOTHER CLASSROOM...

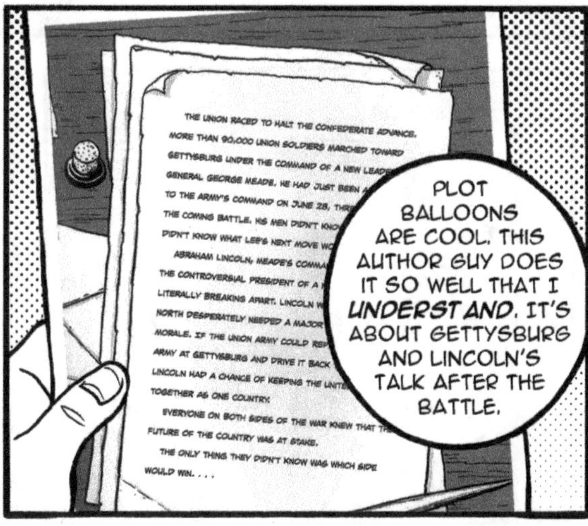

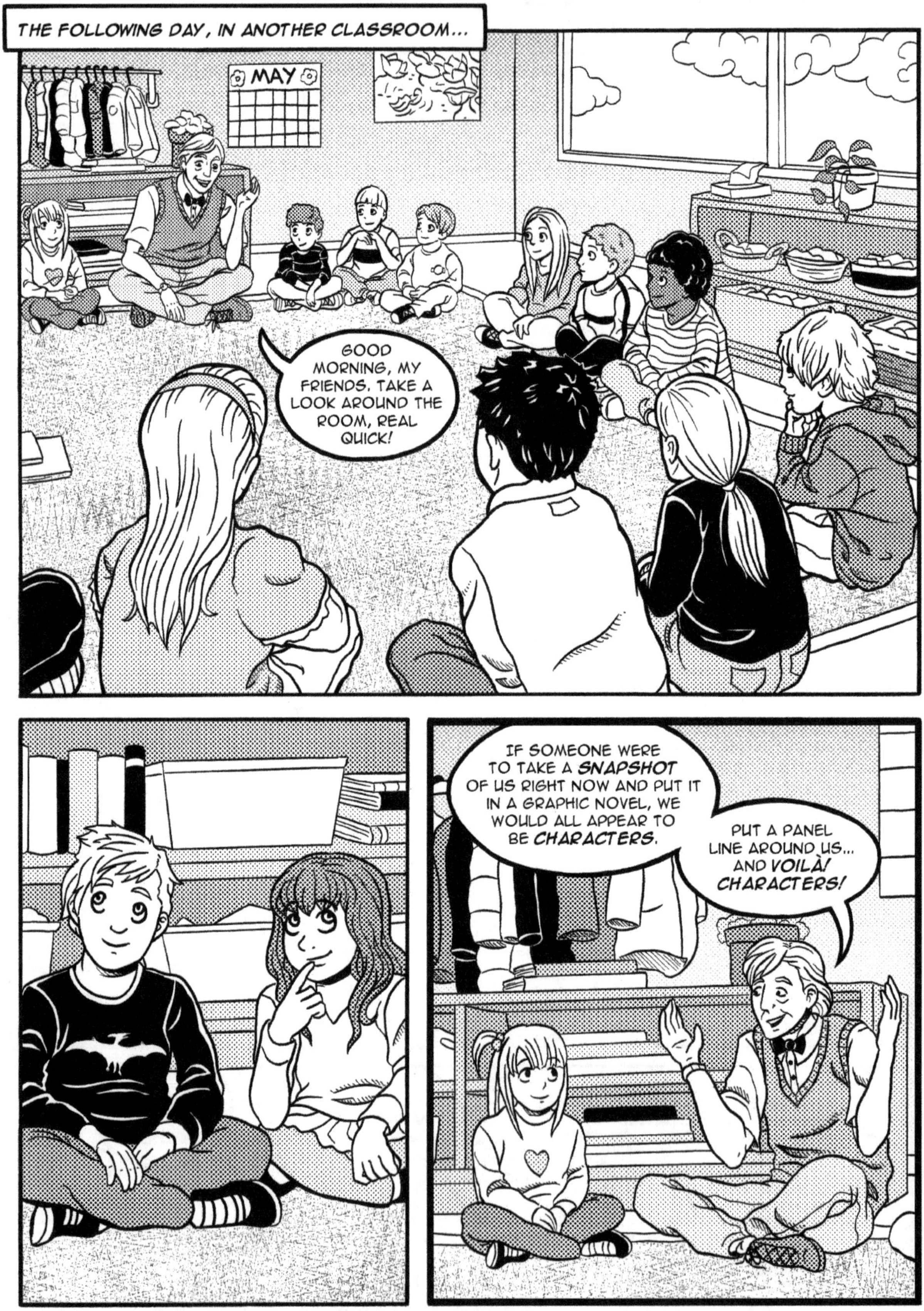

THE FOLLOWING DAY, IN ANOTHER CLASSROOM...

GOOD MORNING, MY FRIENDS. TAKE A LOOK AROUND THE ROOM, REAL QUICK!

Summer Books I Want to Read!

1. *The Giver* by Lois Lowry
2. The *Amulet* series by Kazu Kibuishi
3. A book with snakes found in North America
4. *The Devil's Arithmetic* by Jane Yolen

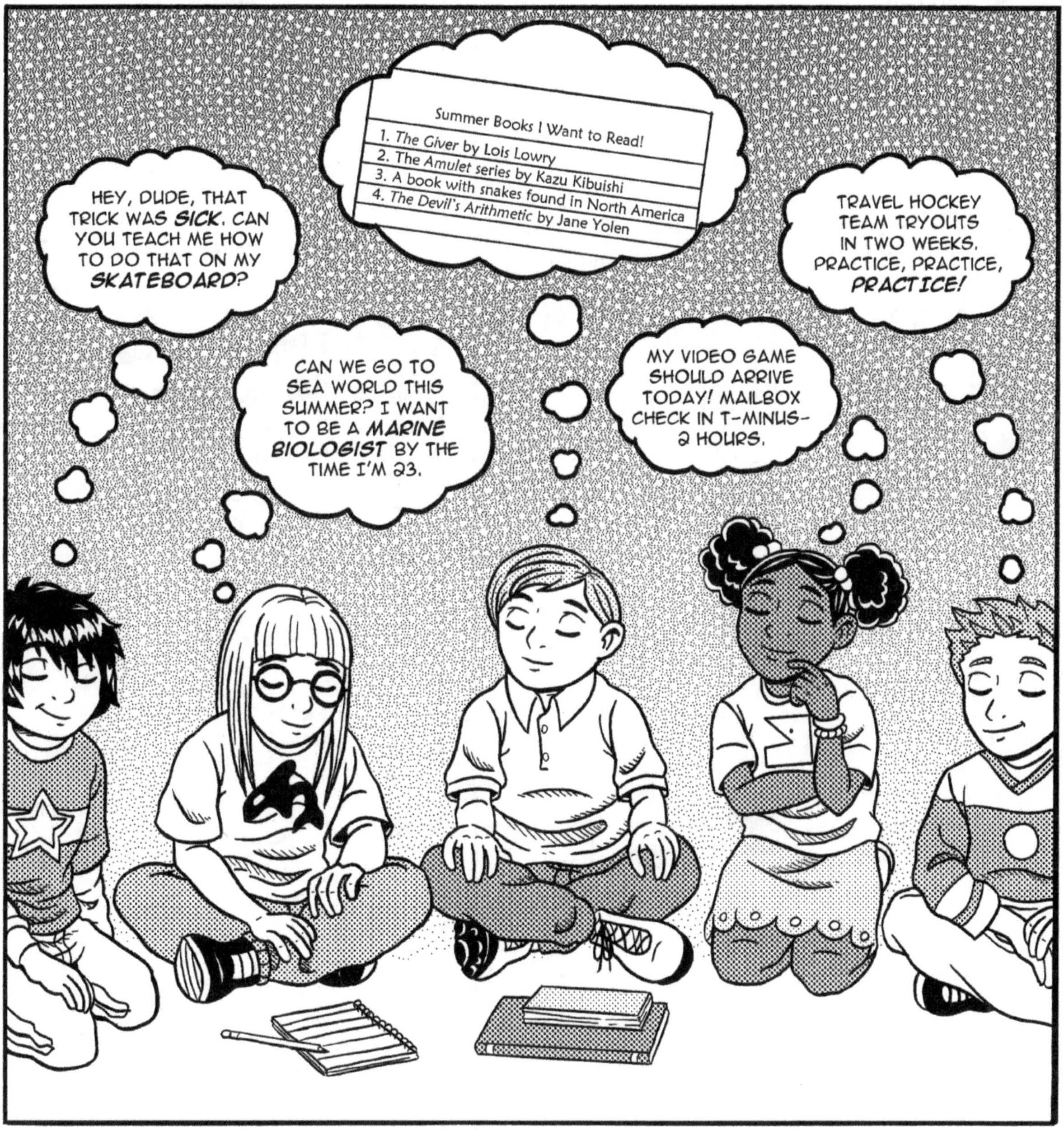

HEY, DUDE, THAT TRICK WAS ***SICK***. CAN YOU TEACH ME HOW TO DO THAT ON MY ***SKATEBOARD***?

TRAVEL HOCKEY TEAM TRYOUTS IN TWO WEEKS. PRACTICE, PRACTICE, ***PRACTICE!***

CAN WE GO TO SEA WORLD THIS SUMMER? I WANT TO BE A ***MARINE BIOLOGIST*** BY THE TIME I'M 23.

MY VIDEO GAME SHOULD ARRIVE TODAY! MAILBOX CHECK IN T-MINUS-2 HOURS.

SKATE

HEY, RACHEL, YOU THINK YOU COULD OUTLINE THE ***VARIOUS TYPES*** OF GRAPHIC NOVEL BALLOONS BEFORE WE GO ON TO THE NEXT CHAPTER?

NO PROBLEM, KATIE!

GRAPHIC NOVEL BALLOONS

ARE USUALLY FOUND INSIDE OF A PANEL AND CREATE VISUAL BOUNDARIES THAT TYPICALLY CONTAIN TEXTUAL ELEMENTS OR INDICATORS CRITICAL TO THE STORY.

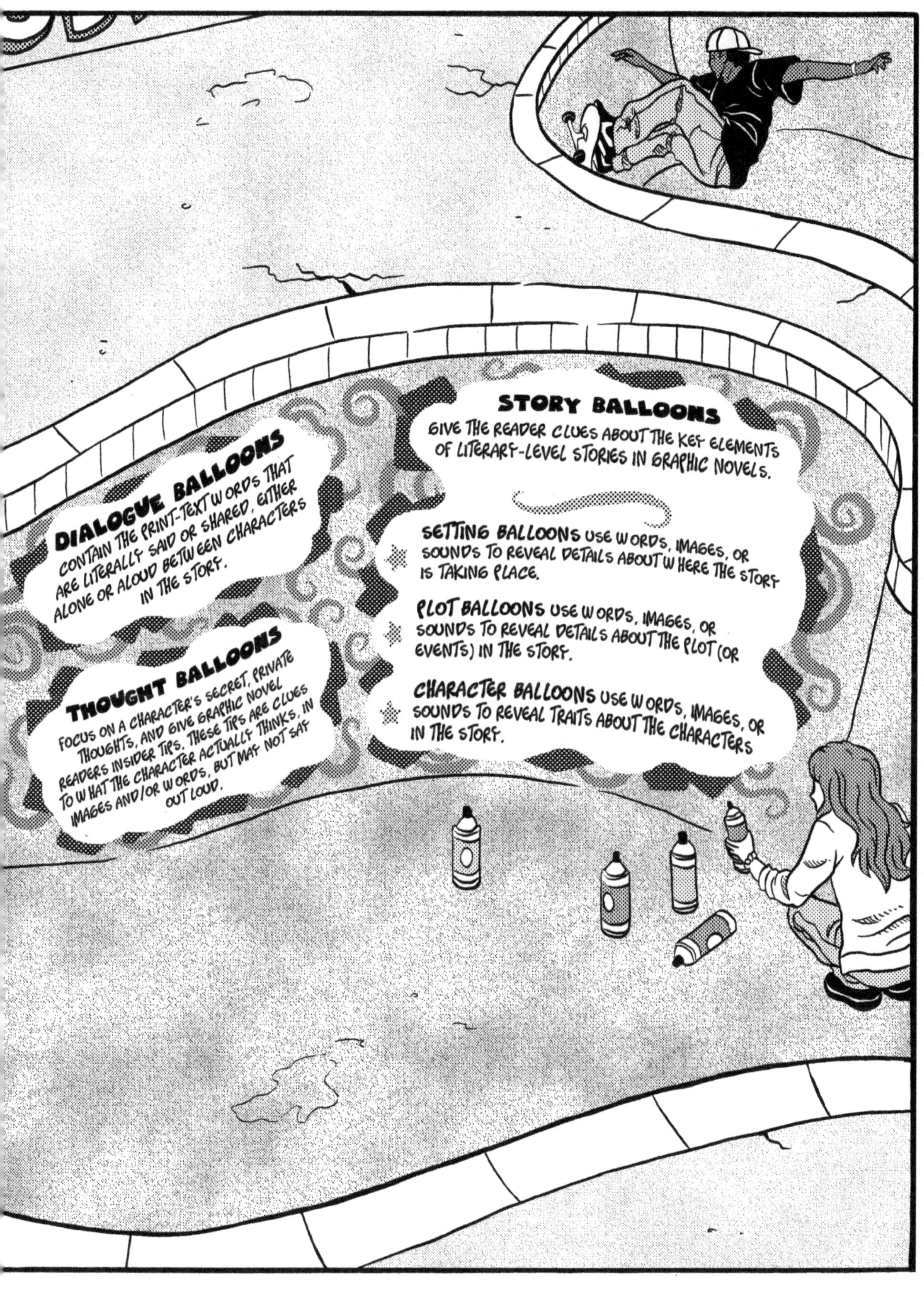

DIALOGUE BALLOONS CONTAIN THE PRINT-TEXT WORDS THAT ARE LITERALLY SAID OR SHARED, EITHER ALONE OR ALOUD BETWEEN CHARACTERS IN THE STORY.
THOUGHT BALLOONS FOCUS ON A CHARACTER'S SECRET, PRIVATE THOUGHTS, AND GIVE GRAPHIC NOVEL READERS INSIDER TIPS. THESE TIPS ARE CLUES TO WHAT THE CHARACTER ACTUALLY THINKS, IN IMAGES AND/OR WORDS, BUT MAY NOT SAY OUT LOUD.
STORY BALLOONS
GIVE THE READER CLUES ABOUT THE KEY ELEMENTS OF LITERARY-LEVEL STORIES IN GRAPHIC NOVELS.
SETTING BALLOONS USE WORDS, IMAGES, OR SOUNDS TO REVEAL DETAILS ABOUT WHERE THE STORY IS TAKING PLACE.
PLOT BALLOONS USE WORDS, IMAGES, OR SOUNDS TO REVEAL DETAILS ABOUT THE PLOT (OR EVENTS) IN THE STORY.
CHARACTER BALLOONS USE WORDS, IMAGES, OR SOUNDS TO REVEAL TRAITS ABOUT THE CHARACTERS IN THE STORY.

RECORD YOUR THOUGHTS

When originally planning and outlining for this book, I kept struggling with all the terminology that currently circulates regarding some of the more unique features found in graphic texts. As we dive deeper and move beyond the fundamentals of graphic texts (like panels, gutters, and balloons), we must continue to think about all of the various and unique ways graphic texts present their stories. As I took notes and listed the features I wanted to point out in this final chapter, my list got longer and longer. I even kept drawing arrows from terms that meant the same thing but various scholars had labeled differently. Synonymous terminology was everywhere. Rather than make predictions about what exact terminology teachers should embrace, I decided to focus this last chapter on continuing the conversation about reading with graphic texts.

So while our current conversation in this book must inevitably have a stopping point, I would like for this chapter to also serve as a platform to encourage future conversation and thought about teaching reading with graphic texts. For that reason, this final chapter considers the future of teaching graphic texts and presents some of the key terms teachers will want to know in order to further empower students to read these popular twenty-first-century texts.

Throughout my ten-plus years of teaching graphic texts, I have consistently come back to one key question regarding the future of reading with graphic texts: *Once teachers and students understand the history and key, foundational terms involved in reading graphic texts, what comes next?*

Because graphic texts have proven to be just as literary and substantial as some of the most famous and well-respected canonical novels of all time, teachers and students need to know how to further decode and dive into this complex literary format.

The next layer is what I like to refer to as "graphic text special effects." And although I throw that term out there very boldly, I believe that it is currently the most familiar term we can build from as we continue to teach literary-level graphic novels. Graphic text special effects rely on a variety of unique literary features to enhance the reader's experience.

POOL RULES
HOURS 10-10

AS WE DIVE DEEPER INTO THE EXCITING AND NEW COMPLEXITIES FOUND IN GRAPHIC TEXTS, WE MUST IMAGINE ***OURSELVES*** AS PART OF THE CONVERSATION.

PLEASE JOIN US!

HAVE A SEAT.

THIS IS GREAT! THE MORE, THE MERRIER!

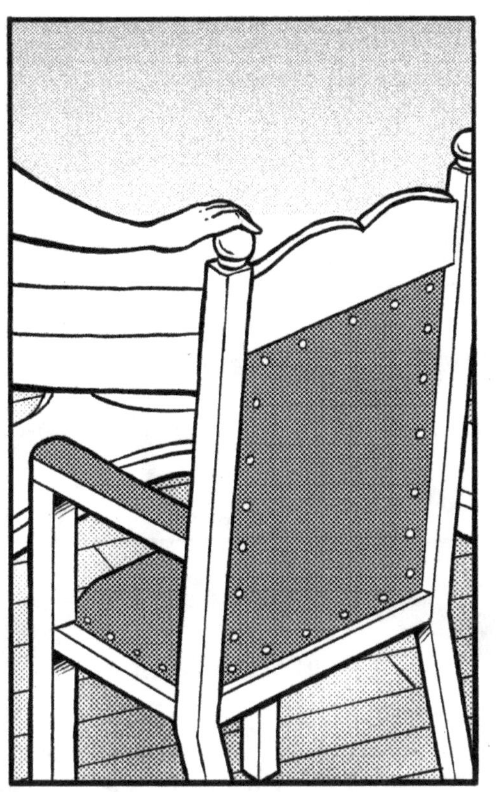

The 5 Key Graphic Text Special Effects

1. The Bifocal Effect
2. The eyeDrive Effect
3. The Scribe Effect
4. The Artist Effect
5. The Stage Effect (foreground and background)

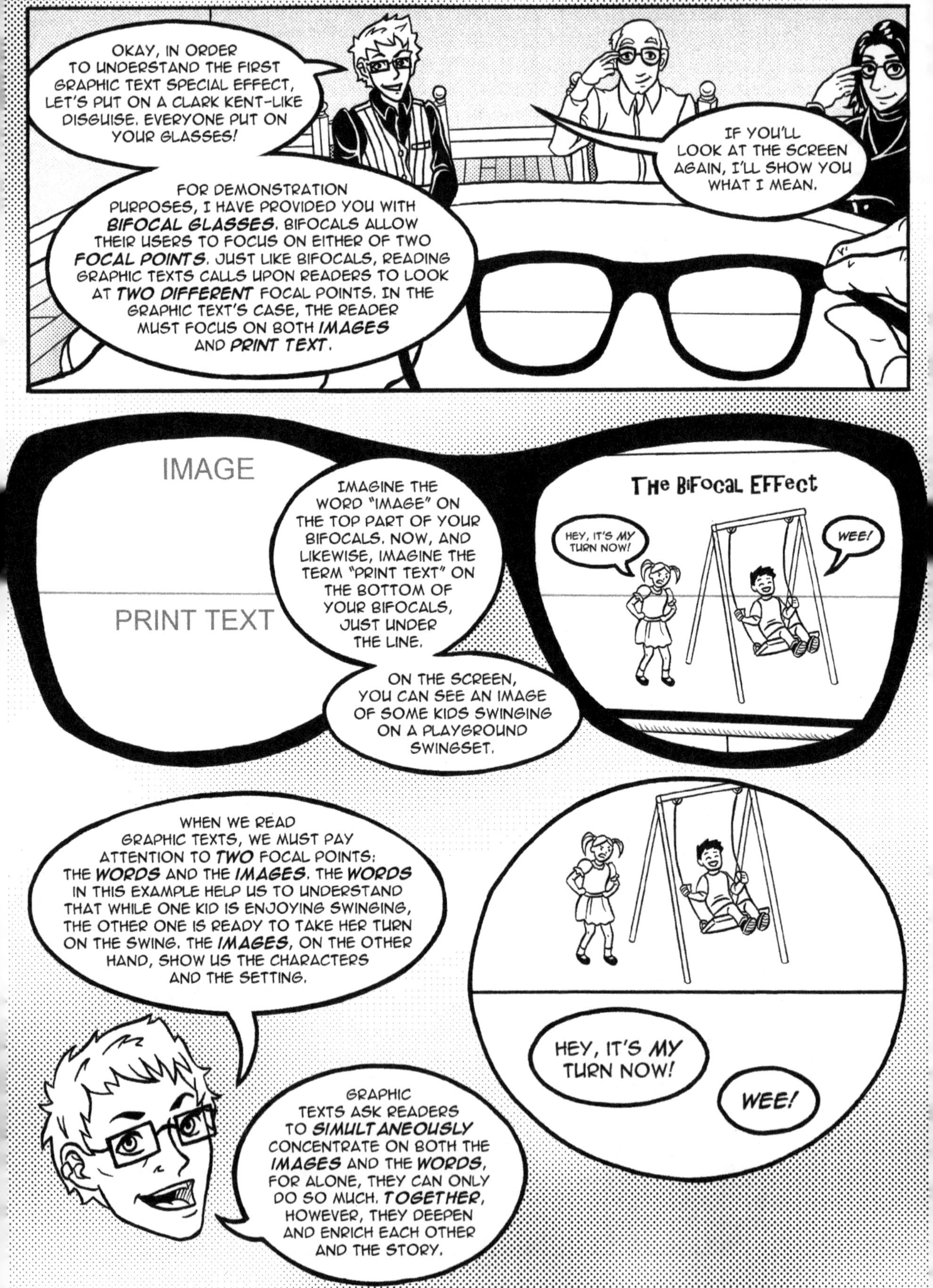

IMAGE

PRINT TEXT

IMAGINE THE WORD "IMAGE" ON THE TOP PART OF YOUR BIFOCALS. NOW, AND LIKEWISE, IMAGINE THE TERM "PRINT TEXT" ON THE BOTTOM OF YOUR BIFOCALS, JUST UNDER THE LINE.

ON THE SCREEN, YOU CAN SEE AN IMAGE OF SOME KIDS SWINGING ON A PLAYGROUND SWINGSET.

The BiFocal EFFect

HEY, IT'S *MY* TURN NOW!

WEE!

WHEN WE READ GRAPHIC TEXTS, WE MUST PAY ATTENTION TO ***TWO*** FOCAL POINTS: THE ***WORDS*** AND THE ***IMAGES***. THE ***WORDS*** IN THIS EXAMPLE HELP US TO UNDERSTAND THAT WHILE ONE KID IS ENJOYING SWINGING, THE OTHER ONE IS READY TO TAKE HER TURN ON THE SWING. THE ***IMAGES***, ON THE OTHER HAND, SHOW US THE CHARACTERS AND THE SETTING.

GRAPHIC TEXTS ASK READERS TO ***SIMULTANEOUSLY*** CONCENTRATE ON BOTH THE ***IMAGES*** AND THE ***WORDS***, FOR ALONE, THEY CAN ONLY DO SO MUCH. ***TOGETHER***, HOWEVER, THEY DEEPEN AND ENRICH EACH OTHER AND THE STORY.

HEY, IT'S *MY* TURN NOW!

WEE!

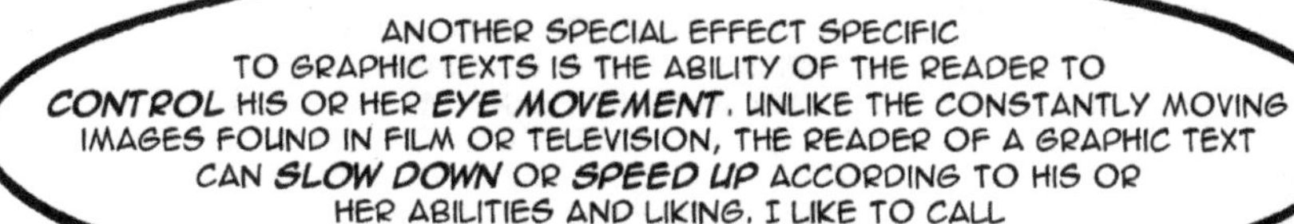

WHEN WE FOLLOW THE HARE, WE ***REACT*** TO HIS SPEED AND OUR EYES WANT TO ***SPEED UP***. WHEN WE FOLLOW THE TORTOISE, THOUGH, OUR READING ***SLOWS DOWN*** WITH HIM, STICKING WITH HIS PACE.

IN GRAPHIC TEXTS THE ***ARTWORK*** OFTEN INFORMS HOW FAST OR SLOW TO READ. AS WE CAN SEE IN THE VERTICAL SPEECH BALLOONS FROM THE SQUIRREL FIRING THE START GUN, THE IMAGES TELL OUR EYE WHICH DIRECTION TO READ: TOP TO BOTTOM, LEFT TO RIGHT.

AFTER YOU JOINED THE LEAGUE, YOU RETURNED TO YOUR CLASSROOM READY TO SHARE THAT NEXT LEVEL OF READING COMPREHENSION AND DECODE GRAPHIC TEXT SPECIAL EFFECTS. OVER TIME, THE MESSAGE ABOUT DIVING DEEPER INTO THE SPECIAL EFFECTS FOUND IN GRAPHIC NOVELS WILL BECOME EVEN MORE EXCITING AND MORE ENCOURAGING REGARDING THE FUTURE OF TEACHING READING IN THE 21ST CENTURY.

TWO MORE GRAPHIC TEXT SPECIAL EFFECTS I LEARNED ABOUT AND WANT TO SHARE WITH YOU ARE: THE SCRIBE EFFECT AND THE ARTIST EFFECT.
THE SCRIBE EFFECT DEALS WITH THE FONT AND LETTERING STYLE USED IN THE GRAPHIC NOVEL. FOR INSTANCE, LOOK AT THE EXAMPLE IN THE GRAPHIC NOVEL I JUST HANDED OUT.

YOU'LL PROBABLY RECOGNIZE THE FONT OR LETTERING STYLE TO BE VERY LIGHT AND FLOWING, ALMOST AS IF IT IS AIRY AND ABLE TO FLY. MIRRORING THE SUPERHERO'S ABILITY TO FLY, THE LETTERING EMPHASIZES AND REINFORCES HIS MOST IMPORTANT POWER.
The Scribe Effect
HEEELP!
WORLD NEWS
I am coming, citizen!

ALONG WITH THE SCRIBE EFFECT, READERS OF GRAPHIC NOVELS WILL ALSO NEED TO BE AWARE OF THE ARTIST EFFECT. JUST LIKE SCRIBES, ARTISTS LIKE TO USE ARTISTIC FEATURES THAT COMPLEMENT THEIR STORY. TURN YOUR SCRIBE EFFECT HANDOUT OVER, AND YOU WILL FIND AN EXAMPLE OF THE ARTIST EFFECT.
The Artist Effect

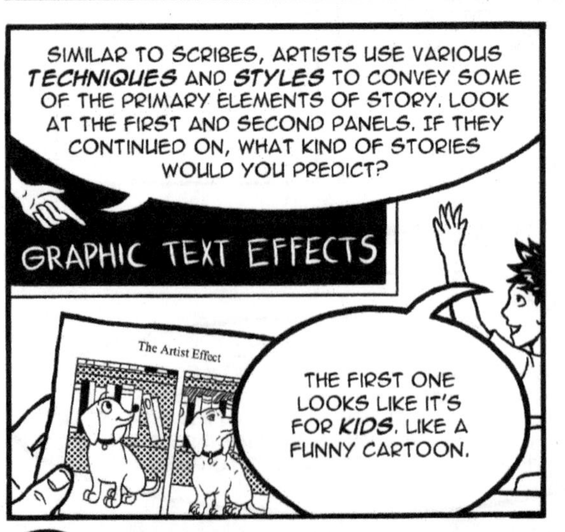
SIMILAR TO SCRIBES, ARTISTS USE VARIOUS TECHNIQUES AND STYLES TO CONVEY SOME OF THE PRIMARY ELEMENTS OF STORY. LOOK AT THE FIRST AND SECOND PANELS. IF THEY CONTINUED ON, WHAT KIND OF STORIES WOULD YOU PREDICT?
GRAPHIC TEXT EFFECTS
The Artist Effect
THE FIRST ONE LOOKS LIKE IT'S FOR KIDS. LIKE A FUNNY CARTOON.

GREAT! I COMPLETELY AGREE. THIS ARTIST IS BEING WHIMSICAL AND FUN, VERY CARTOONISH. WHAT ABOUT THAT SECOND PANEL'S ARTWORK? WHAT DOES IT TELL YOU?
THAT ONE'S MORE SERIOUS. COULD BE THAT THE DOG IS HANGING OUT IN FRONT OF THE BOOKSHELF TO GUARD SOMETHING ON IT.
INTERESTING! AND, YES, IT IS SERIOUS. COULD VERY WELL BE THE DOG ISGUARDING SOMETHING REALLY IMPORTANT.

Graphic Text Special Effects

ANYTHING INTERESTING AT SCHOOL TODAY?
KIND OF.
SOUNDS LIKE A "YES" TO ME!

Graphic Text Special Effects
1. The Bifocal Effect
HOLD ON A SEC. I'LL SHOW YOU.

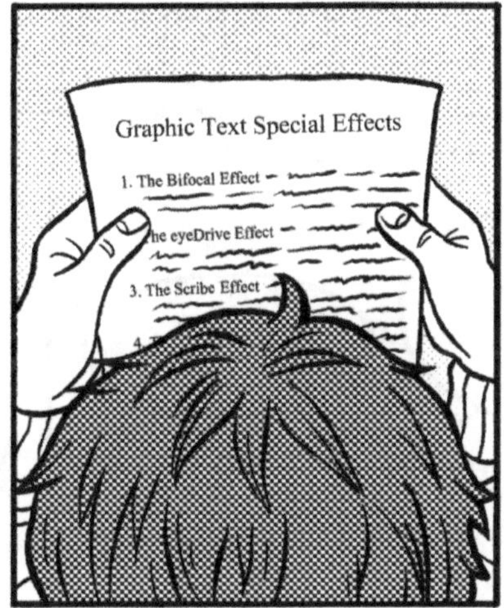
Graphic Text Special Effects
1. The Bifocal Effect
3. The Scribe Effect

WHATCHA GOT THERE?

THE TEACHER HAD SOME NEW STUFF TO TALK ABOUT TODAY. WE ARE READING A GRAPHIC NOVEL, AND SHE TOLD US ABOUT SPECIAL EFFECTS.
LIKE IN THE MOVIES?
SORT OF, BUT THESE ARE FOR GRAPHIC NOVELS. SHE SAID THE MAIN IDEA IS THE SAME THOUGH.

CAN YOU REMEMBER ANY COOL ONES?
UH, WELL, I REALLY THOUGHT THE STAGE EFFECT WAS COOL. MAKES ME THINK OF MOVIES OR TV. IT'S ON MY HANDOUT. I CAN READ IT TO YOU....

"GRAPHIC TEXT PANELS, THE INDIVIDUAL BOUNDARIES THAT EACH CONTAIN A PART OF THE STORY, ALSO HAVE IMPORTANT INFORMATION IN THE **FOREGROUND** OF THE PANEL (LIKE THE **MAIN FOCUS**)."
WHAT WAS COOL IS THAT THEY HAVE A **BACKGROUND**, TOO, WHICH IS REALLY IMPORTANT.
WHAT'S SO GREAT ABOUT THE **BACKGROUND**?
raphic Text Sp ial Effects
e Bifocal Effect - Graphic texts ask readers
ltaneously concentrate on both the images and
rds, for alone, they can only do so much.
er, however, they deepen and enrich each other
story.
eyeDrive Effect - The ability of
l his or her eye movement. Unlike the
ly moving images found in film or telev
er of a graphic text can slow down or speed
g to his or her abilities and liking.
Scribe Effect - deals with the font and
style used in the graphic novel.

THE **STAGE EFFECT** IN GRAPHIC TEXTS IS COOL. IT'S LIKE WHEN YOU READ GRAPHIC NOVELS, EACH OF THE PANELS IS ITS OWN **STAGE**.
THERE'S AN **EMPHASIS** ON THE MAIN FOCUS, WHAT MY TEACHER SAID WAS THE **FOREGROUND**, BUT THERE ARE ALSO DETAILS IN THE **BACKGROUND**. SO WE MUST REMEMBER TO LOOK AT **BOTH**.

IMAGINE, DAD, THAT WE ARE WATCHING A MOVIE OR PLAY AND SOMEONE IS WALKING DOWN A SIDEWALK, NOT NOTICING THAT A **ZOMBIE** IS PEEKING OUT FROM BEHIND A TRASH CAN **BEHIND** HIM.
WOW, THAT'S PRETTY SMART.
YEP. I HAVE TO PAY A LOT OF ATTENTION TO **REALLY UNDERSTAND** WHAT'S GOING ON IN THE FOREGROUND AND BACKGROUND. IF I DON'T, I MIGHT **MISS** SOMETHING.
LIKE, IF I **DIDN'T** NOTICE THE ZOMBIE, IT WOULD REALLY **SURPRISE** ME LATER. BUT THE ARTIST GIVES ME A **HEADS UP** IN THE BACKGROUND SO THAT I KNOW TO LOOK FOR **THAT** JUST AS MUCH AS I LOOK AT THE FOREGROUND.

EVEN **I** KNEW THAT. MY CLASS IS READING **EXTREME BABYMOUSE**, AND WE LOOK AT **EVERYTHING**, NOT JUST THE CHARACTER OR BIG THING ON THE PAGE.
WOW, KIDS! SEEMS LIKE YOUR TEACHERS REALLY UNDERSTAND THESE NEW **GRAPHIC NOVELS** I KEEP SEEING IN BOOKSTORES AND ONLINE. I'M JUST GLAD YOU ARE BOTH STARTING TO **ENJOY READING**. THUMBS UP TO YOUR TEACHERS!

RECORD YOUR THOUGHTS

ALTHOUGH GRAPHIC NOVELS MAY SEEM NEW TO US IN THE 21ST CENTURY, HERE'S A FINAL THOUGHT ON THE SIGNIFICANT EVOLUTION OF GRAPHIC TEXT OVER TIME.
CAVEMAN DAYS
PRE-15TH CENTURY
AH-HA!
15TH-CENTURY INVENTION OF THE PRINTING PRESS
1600S-1800S
1800-1910 INDUSTRIAL REVOLUTION
1920S -1930S
BREAKING NEWS
WAR!
Japan bombs Pearl Harbor
DECEMBER 7, 1941

WHO ARE YOUR FAVORITE TELEVISION CHARACTERS?
The Devil's Arithmetic
Jane Yolen
LOL
TV
1970S
1990S
2010
1980S
BILL
STEVE
TODAY!
GRAPHIC NOVELS ARE PRETTY AWESOME. THEIR POTENTIAL TO USE IMAGES AND WORDS TOGETHER TO TELL A STORY IS LIMITLESS.
SEPTEMBER 11, 2001
BREAKING NEWS
1950S
GREAT EXPECTATIONS
CHARLES DICKENS

SUGGESTED PROFESSIONAL RESOURCES

Bitz, M. (2009). *Manga high: Literacy, identity, and coming of age in an urban high school.*
Cambridge, MA: Harvard Education Press.

Bitz, M. (2010). *When commas meet kryptonite: Classroom lessons from the comic book project.*
New York, NY: Teachers College.

Carter, J. B. (2007). *Building literacy connections with graphic novels: Page by page, panel by panel.*
Urbana, IL: NCTE.

Carter, J.B. (2011). *Super-powered word study: Teaching words and word parts through comics.*
Gainesville, FL: Maupin House.

Eisner, W. (1978). *A contract with God.*
New York, NY: Poorhouse Press.

Eisner, W. (1985). *Comics and sequential art: Principles and practices from the legendary cartoonist.*
New York, NY: Poorhouse Press.

Eisner, W. (1995). *Graphic storytelling and visual narrative.*
New York, NY: Poorhouse Press.

Fehlman, R. H. (1992). *"Making meanings visible: Critically reading TV."*
The English Journal, 81(7), 19-24.

Hajdu, D. (2008). *The ten-cent plague: The great comic-book scare and how it changed America.*
New York, NY: Farrar, Straus, and Giroux.

Kist, W. (2004). *New literacies in action: Teaching and learning in multiple media.*
New York, NY: Teachers College Press.

Kist, W. (2009). *The socially networked classroom: Teaching in the new media age.*
Thousand Oaks, CA: Corwin.

Kress, G. (2003). *Literacy in the new media age.*
New York, NY: Routledge.

Masterman, L. (1985). *Teaching the media.*
New York, NY: Routledge.

McCloud, S. (2006). *Making comics: Storytelling secrets of comics, manga and graphic novels.*
New York, NY: HarperCollins.

McCloud, S. (2000). *Reinventing comics: How imagination and technology are revolutionizing an art form.*
New York, NY: HarperCollins.

McCloud, S. (1993). *Understanding comics: The invisible art.*
New York, NY: HarperCollins.

The Central Advisory Council for Education. (1963). *Half our future.*
London, England: HMSO.

Jaffe, M., Monnin, K. (2012). *Using content-area graphic texts for learning.*
Gainesville, FL: Maupin House.

Monnin, K. (2011). *Teaching early reader comics and graphic novels.*
Gainesville, FL: Maupin House.

Monnin, K. (2009). *Teaching graphic novels: Practical strategies for the secondary ELA classroom.*
Gainesville, FL: Maupin House.

The New London Group. (1996). *"A pedagogy of multi-literacies: Designing social futures."*
Harvard Educational Review, 66(1), 60-92.

Pekar, H. (2005). *Best of American splendor.*
New York, NY: Ballantine.

Pekar, H. (2012). *Harvey Pekar's Cleveland.*
Marietta, GA: Top Shelf.

Satrapi, M. (2007). *The complete Persepolis.*
New York, NY: Pantheon.

Smith, J. (2005). *Bone, vol. 1: Out from Boneville.*
New York, NY: Scholastic.

Spiegelman, A. (2003). *Maus: A survivor's tale.*
New York, NY: Penguin Books.

Wertham, F. (1954). *Seduction of the innocent.*
New York, NY: Reinhart.

NOTES!